PICTORIAL HISTORY OF
AMERICA'S RAILROADS

PICTORIAL HISTORY OF
AMERICA'S RAILROADS

Mike Del Vecchio

MBI Publishing Company

DEDICATION

To my parents, Mike and Carol, for their patience and love.

In memory of Jeff Woosnam, a fellow journalist and good friend whose half-century of colorful words and wisdom were lost much too soon.

5109: Railroads Across America

Produced by Quadrillion Publishing Limited, Godalming Business Centre, Woolsack Way, Godalming GU7 1XW, UK

This edition first published in 1998 by MBI Publishing Company, 729 Prospect Avenue, PO Box 1, Osceola, WI 54020-0001 USA

MBI Publishing Company books are also available at discounts in bulk quantity for industrial or sales-promotional use. For details write to Special Sales Manager at Motorbooks International Wholesalers & Distributors, 729 Prospect Avenue, PO Box 1, Osceola, WI 54020-0001 USA

Library of Congress Cataloging-in-Publication Data Available
ISBN 0-7603-0829-2

Printed in Hong Kong by Dai Nippon Co. (HK) Ltd.

CREDITS

Commissioning editors: Will Steeds and Chris Stone
Project manager: Christopher Westhorp
Design: Peter Laws and Mark Holt
Picture research: Tony Moore
Index: Chris Bernstein
Color reproduction: Dai Nippon Printing Co. (HK) Ltd.

CONTENTS

FOREWORD

America grew up along the railroad. Even though today's kids see mostly malls and mini-marts and eight-lane highways with concrete sound barriers, the real America of the past century developed around the railroad station and grain elevator and a whistle in the night. The cities were made possible by trains carrying commuters long before the commuters carried computers. Today it is suburbia, the inner city and pickup trucks and "road rage" that show up on cable television and the Internet.

But not too long ago, America moved on rails, and trains shaped the country that we know today. It was railroads bringing in coal that made modern cities possible by providing relatively clean heat, and those same railroads brought refrigerator cars into the warehouse districts where local merchants could get fresh produce for their customers. And the railroads linked the mines to the steel mills and those mills to the fabricating plants and automobile factories. When the endurance of a horse and wagon determined the distance between communities and the size of a farmer's field, the railroads threw down a steel network that tied the country together with arteries of rapid commerce.

No longer was geography a barrier to the human spirit. Many a weary young farmhand gave up the plow for the coal scoop on a steam locomotive and a chance to charge across the amber waves of grain at a mile a minute. The image of the railroad is the image of America in its innocent youth and lusty adolescence.

Today the railroad is harder to see in everyday life. Commuter trains are modern and efficient, and mile-long unit coal trains supply the power plants, far from public view. But double-stack container trains still reach across the country carrying everything from your new Toyota to breakfast orange juice.

The image of the railroad is the image of America. And this book demonstrates the strength, beauty and sheer diversity of that image over the years.

Jim Boyd
Newton, New Jersey
July 23, 1998

PREFACE

No one more than 150 years ago could have predicted how big and how important—and how profitable—railroading would become. It always amazes me how many of the early traditions are still followed today, both on the railroad and in much of the speech of the non-rail-oriented citizen.

But today railroading has improved to where it is hauling the most tonnage in history with the fewest locomotives and employees. Railroading is not the huge employer it was during the steam era. Yet the raw materials for almost everything in any department or grocery store got there by train. Even the passenger trains are thriving. Around New York City alone the commuter railroads carry nearly 750,000 riders each day, while the New York Subway System carries four million.

Books three times the size of this one have tried to tell the entire tale and failed. We have endeavored to cover many of the important sights and events. The editors and I have divided the book into three sections covering three eras. Within these sections, the chapters are organized geographically. A trip through a century-and-a-half of railroading has certainly been a fun and diverse ride. We hope you enjoy it, too.

Mike Del Vecchio
Dover, New Jersey
July 1998

PART ONE
1
THE EARLY DAYS

The young George Stephenson in the 1780s would watch the passing trains of horse-drawn wagons loaded with coal from the mines near Newcastle, England. It was on these parallel wooden timbers that the railroad industry was effectively born. For, inspired, Stephenson would later design steam locomotives; since then, railroading has grown in leaps and bounds to carry people and commerce—and the industrial revolution—over its steel ribbons. By 1830 it had spread to America; private investment and enterprise added thousands of miles each year and grew the steam locomotive from the primitive, diminutive engines imported from England to the massive machines that impressed the world 100 years later.

The Civil War taught North America that the railroads needed to be operated as a coherent network. Railroads were soon built to a standard gauge; numerous inventions followed which helped to make trains longer, faster and safer.

To assist expansion westward the government awarded land on which to build track and towns to lure settlers. In 1869, iron rails spanned America for the first time. The railroads had industrialized the East, and now they took on the task of settling the West. Railroading was growing—but, back then, few could have predicted just how big it would become.

AN INDUSTRY IS BORN

It is difficult today to imagine a world without railways, as nearly every facet of our lives is tied to the railroad industry in some way. In North America, the railroads are moving more tonnage than ever before with 6000 horse power (hp) locomotives that only visit the shop once in four months. But this wasn't always the case. At the beginning of the nineteenth century, railroads were a novelty that a few coal mines had tried in an effort to get more tonnage out of the mine with the same mule. But precisely where and when railroading was born was, is, and will continue to be debated among historians.

The concept of what we consider today to be railways can be traced back thousands of years to the Egyptians and the construction of the Great Pyramids. Many of the large stones used to build those monuments were transported on logs that rolled in guideways built of stone. The Egyptian engineers understood the advantages of a hard surface: heavy loads could be dragged over it with minimal work. The same hard surface advantages were exploited by the engineers of the Roman Empire when they were constructing the famed Appian Way. Chariots rolled like streetcars over this most famous of early thoroughfares. Essentially, it was the making of a roadway that led to the invention of the railway.

AN INDUSTRY IS BORN

Railways and railroading were born in England. Early railways, dating to 1630, were used for the transport of coal; they were constructed of smooth wooden planks for rails that rested on supporting wooden sleepers, and the pulley-like shaped wheel treads rolled on a half-round, wooden molding-like surface nailed to the top of the rails.

The first written accounts of iron rails tell of their use in 1740 at Whitehaven, Cumberland. The rails were iron moldings, and proved to be far superior to wood moldings in withstanding wear. In 1789 in Loughborough, Leicestershire, William Jessop built a railway using cast-edge rail, with flanges cast onto the wheels. This is the first recorded use of the flanged wheel—the very basis of railroading. It didn't take long for the commercial collieries of England to produce edge rails; such early iron rails were narrow at the base and widened toward the top. Introduced in 1808, this type of rail was produced until the late 1820s, when machinery was invented that would roll rails into a shape more like that we know today. The technology of the time only permitted rails to be cast in three- or four-foot lengths. Thus the track required numerous joints. Motive power up to this time was still provided by horse, mule or human.

Track construction advanced just as significantly as the wheel. In 1800 in Derbyshire, Benjamin Outram introduced the use of stone sleepers, or props, to support the ends of the wooden rails at the joining or plank end. Drastically different in appearance from the conventional wood road, this new construction became known as the "Outram Road," which in time simply became known as a "Tram Road," though that term would later fit a broader description of a railway.

LOCOMOTION

Much has been written about the invention of the steam engine, and it is commonly accepted that Thomas Newcomen was the first person to patent a steam engine design, in 1705. He was using this engine to pump water out of mines by 1710. By 1759, James Watt had learned of Newcomen's work; Watt made his first steam engine in 1769, or slightly later. The steam engine designed by Newcomen was a condensing engine; steam would force the piston in one direction, and a jet of cold water would cool the cylinder, thus causing a vacuum that sucked the piston back up. Watt later discovered that steam is more powerful when it expands, and he improved his engine accordingly. In 1784 he made public his engine that used steam to move the piston in both directions. But boats were the first vehicles to receive steam engines, and there are accounts of steam engines in ships as early as 1759 in France.

Across the Atlantic in the United States, the wealthy Revolutionary War Colonel John Stevens of

Hoboken, New Jersey, experimented with steam-powered vessels as early as 1791 on the Hudson River. Stevens soon replaced his own horse-powered contraption with one powered by a Watt steam engine. His experiments lasted until 1807, and the Stevens steamboat is said to have traveled at five miles per hour (mph).

Stevens was not the first in the US to build a steamboat, however. Americans named Runsey and Fitch both had designs dating to 1783, and both demonstrated models of them to General George Washington.

The man most often credited with inventing the steamboat, Robert Fulton, began his experiments in France in 1803 upon the River Seine with a small boat driven by side-mounted paddle wheels powered by a Watt steam engine. Fulton returned to America to construct a larger boat of similar design, which he successfully sailed in 1807. While Fulton did not invent the steamboat, he did invent the paddle wheel system of propulsion by steam, a design that endured upon the waters of America. Indeed, as we approach the turn of the twenty-first century, the *Delta Queen*—one of the very last American Civil War-era steam boats still operating—continues to traverse the muddy Mississippi River.

The first steam-powered land vehicle dates to 1769, and was built by Frenchman Nicolas-Joseph Cugnot. His carriage was the first such powered vehicle to travel on public roads. Remarkably, Cugnot's "locomotive", as it was called, is enshrined in the Musée Conservatoire des Arts et Metiers in Paris. The heritage of all the world's steam locomotives can be traced back to this single vehicle.

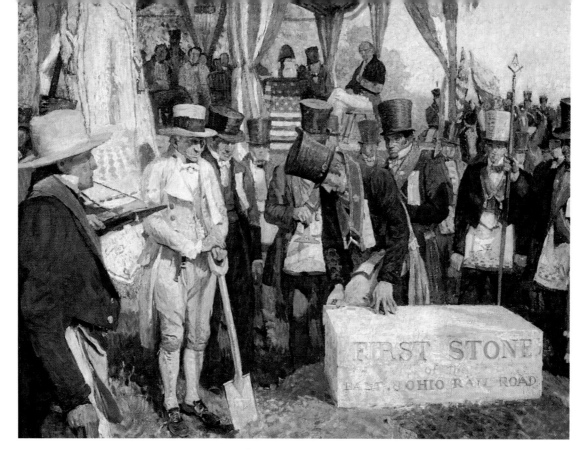

The first record of a British steam carriage dates to 1784: a model built by William Murdock. It was a three-wheeled conveyance that was seen by a Cornish tin mine foreman named Richard Trevithick, who was determined to build a carriage that would not require animals for its power. Trevithick teamed up with a "Mr. Vivian," and they received a patent on their design in 1802.

The pair designed their steam engine to operate solely on high-pressure steam and no vacuum—it used steam to act on the piston in both directions, much as Watt had done. The resulting carriage was demonstrated in London, but the roads were too rough and the men abandoned the project. Trevithick, however, turned his attention back to mining, and he wondered about the use of his carriage on the much smoother tramways at the mines. He built such a machine in 1804 and operated it on the Merthyr-Tydfil Railway in South Wales. It pulled several wagons loaded with ten tons of iron at a stately five mph. Though the exact date is lost to history, it was in South Wales that an industry was born.

Back in the United States, however, there are reports of steam locomotives predating Trevithick's, although none performed feats such as the latter's. For example, the aforementioned John Fitch demonstrated a model of a steam locomotive to George Washington and his cabinet in Philadelphia in the 1780s. Fitch's locomotive operated on a wooden track and was equipped with wheels with outside flanges. Washington was a devotee of canals and, apparently, wasn't impressed. What makes this story credible is the fact that Fitch's locomotive still exists. (The two-foot-square model is at the Ohio State Archeological & Historical Society Museum in Columbus.) It has a copper boiler mounted sideways to the track and a vertical cylinder. It is, perhaps, the most significant railway relic in existence.

THE RAILROAD LOCOMOTIVE IS BORN

While Trevithick's 1804 achievement was significant, his first train was less than perfect in performance. The drivers slipped continually, and in the coming years, others patented many ideas to improve adhesion.

During this time a young man named George Stephenson, the clever and talented son of a poor mining family, had been thinking about building a better steam locomotive. Born in 1781 at Wylam, near Newcastle, Stephenson spent his childhood days watching trains of horse-drawn wagons loaded with coal. At the age of fifteen he got a job as a fireman on the mine's pump engines, spending as much time as he could learning about and repairing the machines. In 1804 he accepted a job in charge of one of Watt's steam engines.

Stephenson's first locomotive was tried on the Killinwood Railway in 1814. Named the Blucher, the locomotive pulled eight loaded wagons of thirty tons each at about four mph. Blucher was the most successful steam locomotive built up to that point. Stephenson patented a second engine during February 1815. It had all four drive wheels connected together. To eliminate mechanical shock from the track, Stephensen invented ball-and-socket joints on the connecting rods. The successes of George Stephenson were by this time becoming well known, both in Britain and in America.

While railroads were common around coal mines at this time, these were separate and individual operations. The idea that railways could connect cities, or be joined to form a network, was still in the future. However, by 1820 there was a fervor rising to build a railroad between Liverpool and Manchester; Stephenson intended to provide the locomotives. In 1824 he became the chief engineer of the Stockton & Darlington Railway, another coal road. The Stockton & Darlington used three Stephenson locomotives and, using Locomotive No.1, Stephenson himself was to demonstrate rail's potential by hauling 600 people from Darlington to Stockton in a little over three hours, including stops. This trip is significant: it was the first time so many passengers had ridden the rails, and it was the first use of a passenger coach on a train. The railroad era as we know it had truly begun. The following month, the passenger coach was put into regular service with much success.

THE RAINHILL TRIALS

In just a few years the plans to build the Liverpool-Manchester railroad took hold, and the directors decided to offer a cash prize for the best locomotive that could meet the minimum requirement. Trials began on October 6, 1828—a day now regarded as representing the beginning of the modern era in railroading. Four locomotives, with their builders, were present in front of thousands of spectators at the town of Rainhill, nine miles east of Liverpool. The four locomotives and builders were The Novelty, built by Messrs. Braithwait and Ericson; The Sans-Pareil, built by Timothy Hockworth; The Rocket, built by Stephenson & Company; and The Perseverance, built by Mr. Burtstall.

Stephenson, of course, had the most experience in steam locomotive design and construction, and his was the only locomotive ready for trial on October 6. His Rocket was an all-new design, and it proved to be his best yet. By the end of the eight-day trials, only his exceeded all eight conditions, including purchase price. Stephenson won the prize—while the United States watched, literally. For several spectators from the US were in attendance at Rainhill. Among them was Horatio Allen, an employee of the Delaware & Hudson Canal Company. Allen had been sent to Rainhill to review the proceedings, with instructions to purchase three steam locomotives for a railway being built between Honesdale and Carbondale, Pennsylvania. Also in attendance was E.L. Miller of the South Carolina Railroad. These two men were to have a profound impact on American railroading.

RAILROADING REACHES THE UNITED STATES

Americans had been following and promoting railway projects in the US, but it was a tough battle since George Washington, and thus Congress, were promoting canal and highway projects to develop the American interior.

BELOW

The Baltimore & Ohio was up and running by 1830. This illustration from 1838 shows that it was the only railroad in town for many years. In fact, Baltimore became one of the most important ports in the US because of the railroad.
Davis Miller, Historical Society of York County, THR Pictures

BELOW

At numerous fairs, expositions, and for motion picture projects, the early scenes along the Baltimore & Ohio Railroad are frequently re-enacted for posterity. The grasshopper-style locomotive and stage coaches on flanged wheels were typical of that era.
AAR photo, MARS

Historians agree that the very first full-size railway in the United States was completed in Quincy, Massachusetts, in 1827. Three miles in length, the road connected granite quarries in Quincy to the Neponset River. It was built with granite sleepers seven-and-a-half foot long and eight foot apart. The pine rails were a foot deep, laid to five-foot gauge and covered with iron strap rail.

America's second railway was built between January and March 1827; a nine-mile line, it connected the coal mines of Mauch Chunk, Pennsylvania, and the Lehigh River. This line was already unusual in that it had a 900-foot inclined plane within a half a mile of the mines. This railway, too, was built on wooden rails clad in strap iron on wooden sleepers.

In 1828 the Delaware & Hudson Canal Company was building its line between the mines at Carbondale and the end of its canal at Honesdale, Pennsylvania. (The same year, the Baltimore & Ohio Railroad and the South Carolina Railroad had also commenced building track.) The Delaware & Hudson Canal Company project has much significance. It attempted to climb up and over the Moosic Mountains by using three inclines and many miles of relatively flat running. The plan was to use locomotives on the flats, and to hoist the empty wagons up the inclines; each locomotive would stay on its assigned level. The Delaware &

Hudson Canal Company construction was the first privately funded capital project in America, worth more than $1 million.

As noted above, the Delaware & Hudson's chief engineer John B. Jervis had sent Horatio Allen to Rainhill to purchase three locomotives, and also to purchase iron rails. He bought the Stourbridge Lion, built by Foster, Rastrick & Company at Stourbridge, England. The price was $2914.90, delivered. Allen also bought a Stephenson-built locomotive named America for $3663.30, delivered, and two sisters to the Lion; one named Delaware and the other named Hudson. On January 15, 1829, the clipper ship *Columbia* delivered the America to New York. It was set up on blocks at Abeel & Dunscomb's foundry at 375 Water Street, to test run under steam. On May 13, 1829, a ship called the *John Jay* arrived in New York harbor with the Lion. The Lion, too, was unloaded, assembled, put up on jacks and run on shop steam for hundreds of onlookers. On July 4, the Lion and the America were shipped with the iron up the Hudson River to Rondout (Kingston), and then south on the Delaware & Hudson Canal to Honesdale. The Lion arrived in Honesdale late in July and was prepared for service.

On August 8, 1829, Horatio Allen drove the Lion back and forth within the town of Honesdale along the banks of the Lackawaxen River. This was the first time that a self-propelled locomotive ran on permanent, purpose-built track in North America, and the townsfolk knew it.

However, the demonstration did not go smoothly. The problem was that the Delaware & Hudson here was laid on hemlock-timber rails and sleepers laid to four-foot three-inch gauge. Horatio Allen himself wrote that "the timber had warped and cracked due to exposure to the sun. The impression was that [the engine] would either break down or it would leave the track on a curve and plunge into the creek." The Lion was heavier than requested—too heavy for the design of the railroad.

The Lion made one more test run on September 9, but the conclusion was the same: the Lion was just too heavy for the track. The locomotive never ran again.

Roseby's Rock—
On Christmas Eve, 1852, the Baltimore and Ohio Linked Baltimore with the Ohio River, thus fulfilling the Original Purpose of Its Founders—

The Delaware & Hudson continued to operate by gravity, and with horses and stationary engines; the Lion was set aside and was gradually dismantled by scavenging locals needing the parts for one reason or another. The boiler was used in a Carbondale foundry for more than two decades after its history-making performance. Eventually, Allen left the Delaware & Hudson for the South Carolina Railroad. What happened to the sisters of the Lion isn't certain.

Despite this setback, the germ of railroad fever was beginning to incubate. On April 27, 1827, a charter to build the Baltimore & Ohio Railroad was granted—this was the first railroad charter to be granted in the United States. The Baltimore & Ohio was also the first railroad to be built for commercial use. With the company officers organized and private money raised, the Baltimore & Ohio Railroad Company broke ground on July 4, 1828, in downtown Baltimore, in front of a grand assemblage. (On that very same July 4, along the shores of the Potomac in Georgetown, the Chesapeake & Ohio Canal Company had also broken ground, backed primarily by government loans and grants. Interestingly, the privately funded Baltimore & Ohio completed a line into Cumberland in 1851, a full eight years before the Chesapeake & Ohio Canal reached that city.) Baltimore & Ohio Railroad rails eventually reached Wheeling, West Virginia, in 1852; at about 300 miles, it was the longest railroad in the world at that time.

The Baltimore & Ohio Railroad Company had originally ordered a British locomotive similar to the Stourbridge Lion to pull its trains. Damaged

during loading in England, the locomotive was never delivered. Some of the railroad's investors had argued that steam locomotives could never be used on the Baltimore & Ohio's route, anyway—for the first thirteen miles between Baltimore and Elicott City circuitously followed the Patapsco River westward, and they were concerned that any locomotive would derail on such trackage.

Peter Cooper, of the Cooper Institute in New York City, rose to the challenge and designed and built an experimental locomotive that he hoped could handle the track's sharp curves. On Saturday, August 28, 1830, Cooper's little engine—nicknamed the Tom Thumb—steamed the entire thirteen miles effortlessly, traversing the 400-foot radius curves and attaining speeds of fifteen mph. One coach with thirty persons on board was in tow. Cooper's engine was reversed and began the trip home, and into history. The biggest stage company in the area at the time was Stockton & Stokes, and one of its stages caught up to Cooper at Relay House on the return trip. According to Baltimore & Ohio Railroad Company attorney H.B. LaTrobe, who was in the coach, "it was at this point it was determined to have a race home." The horse jumped ahead, as the locomotive accelerated slowly. Mr. LaTrobe reported that when the horse was approximately a quarter-mile ahead, Cooper's engine came to life and caught up. "Neck and neck and nose to nose," he added, and the engine passed the horse. Just then a belt that drove the blower that kept draft in the engine broke, and the pressure dropped. Cooper lost the race, but won the contest. His locomotive proved that steam was viable, not only to the Baltimore & Ohio, but to the world. Almost as if inspired by Rainhill, the Baltimore & Ohio Railroad Company officers posted public notice that it would offer a cash prize for the best locomotive design. It had nine criteria by which the machines would be judged. The Baltimore & Ohio was a steam road from then on. In South Carolina another significant railroad project was taking shape. In Charleston, the South Carolina Railroad had advertised for locomotive designs. After considering locomotives that used horses on a treadmill for power, and another with a sail to harness the wind—remarkably, both designs did travel over ten mph—the road opted for a steam locomotive, and accepted an offer of E.L. Miller of Charleston to build a locomotive at the West Point Foundry in New York City.

By this time Horatio Allen was chief engineer of the South Carolina Railroad. Miller traveled to New York to supervise the construction of his locomotive, and he named it the Best Friend. This would be the first locomotive constructed in America for use on a railroad. In October 1830, the Best Friend was loaded on the freight ship *Niagara*, bound for Charleston harbor. During December, the Best Friend was tried, and was faster and pulled more than expected. Then tragedy struck when, in June 1831, the locomotive blew up. (It seems that the fireman, annoyed by the engine's noise, tightened down the safety valve and sat on it to keep it closed. He died from his injuries a few days later.) This event caused the South Carolina Railroad to order from the West Point Foundry the second locomotive built in America for service on an actual railroad. Similar to the Best Friend, but designed by Horatio Allen, it was delivered by the ship *Lafayette* on February 28, 1831.

No description of first locomotives is complete without mention of Colonel John Stevens of Hoboken, who was convinced, almost before anybody else, that steam railroading was the future. To prove it, he built a circle of track in his backyard, and what is most often described as a "model" of a locomotive. It was a four-flanged wheel affair that drove on a geared wheel that meshed with a rack rail underneath. Descriptions call it a model, but a contemporary painting shows the locomotive to be full-sized. Stevens' locomotive operated in 1825, four years before the Stourbridge Lion, and one year before the first American railroad was built.

RAILROAD FEVER

The success of the early railroad companies, and their locomotives, caused a blossoming of the railroad industry. The few lines of just a few miles each grew into a total of 3000 miles of track by the

ABOVE
Railroads would issue passes to employees and officers of the railroad to show to ticket collectors on passenger trains. This example is from the New York & Erie Railroad and is dated June 29, 1859.
Peter Newark's American Pictures

ABOVE
George Pullman created a business empire building sleeping cars. He started in 1858 with financier Benjamin C. Field. They convinced the Chicago & Alton to let them rebuild two day coaches, No.'s 9 and 19, into sleepers. The photo is of a replica of the No.9, built in 1897 for display at the Tennessee Centennial Exposition. In 1948 it was restored for the Chicago Railroad Fair.
Pullman Company, MARS

1840s. As the railroads grew in length and in number, most track and equipment construction followed British practice. But ingenious individuals on several American lines furthered the technology of railroading. First came the track. Early lines, such as the Baltimore & Ohio and the Camden & Amboy, had been built on stone sleepers that supported the rails at each end and at several points in between. The sleepers were laid as a specific gauge and supported heavy timber rails, onto which strap iron was fastened by nails. (This type of track was very similar to British track and the original "Outram" track of the previous century.) The railroads that built all-timber track, with horizontal wood cross-ties supporting the timber rails, had all found that the heavy British locomotives were too much for the structure. During the 1830s and 1840s, most of the iron rails in America were made in England. Railroad builders favored British wrought iron because of its quality, and because it was cheaper than domestic iron. The strap iron system had an inherent flaw, however. As the nail heads wore from use, the strap iron would curl and punch through the floor of the coach. The invention of T-rail was thus a significant development.

Legend has it that T-rail was invented by Robert Stevens (the son of Colonel John Stevens). Robert was whittling while traveling to England to purchase rails for the Camden & Amboy, and tumbled to the I- or T-shaped form. The first boatload of T-rails, 550 pieces, each sixteen-foot long, three inches tall and weighing thirty-six pounds per yard, arrived in Philadelphia in May 1831. Rolled T-rail

has enough girder strength to support the weight of a train, and it can be spiked to the cross-tie from the base. T-rail supported by timber cross-ties was less labor-intensive to construct, and it provided a more versatile track structure.

After the American Civil War, track engineers began placing iron plates between the rail and the cross-tie to spread the weight even further. About this time, track was also being supported in a layer of ballast. Consisting of small stones, or cinders (the after-product of coal burned in locomotives), the ballast helps to spread the weight of the track and the train across a wider area of ground. An added advantage of ballast, it was discovered many years later, is that it allows water to drain away from the cross-ties.

After the Civil War, the Carnegie Steel Works near Pittsburgh developed an economical method of producing steel in large quantities. Orders for rail flooded in, mostly from the rapidly growing Pennsylvania Railroad at first, pushing Carnegie to the top of the steel industry early, although by the 1890s companies such as Bethlehem and Colorado Foundry & Iron were worthy competitors.

STANDARD GAUGE?

By 1883, every railroad in North America considered a distance of four foot eight and one-half inches between the rails to be the "standard gauge." The popular legend (one that promises to be perpetuated into the twenty-first century), was that standard gauge was based on the ruts in the roads left by Roman chariots. This has never been

proven. When railroading began, the distance between the rails was a random decision. Which came first, the gauge or the equipment? Consider that the first railways were simply wooden trackways built under the existing horse-drawn wagons of the time. The flange was on the track, not the wheel. These wagons were likely wearing ruts in the ground over which they traveled, and perhaps the carts bogged down to the point of stalling in wet weather. Okay, the wagons were the source of the gauge of the first railways, but the wagon width was probably as varied as the men who built them. During railroading's genesis, railroads were somewhat of a luxury. Once the efficiencies were discovered, all mines built railways of some sort. The gauge was varied, of course, according to equipment. The wooden railways from the mid-1700s most commonly laid rails at a distance of four foot, for example. But during the early era, men didn't dream that the world would be laced with so many railways. The first rail transportation companies were privately owned; they had to be concerned with competition and they almost all avoided any commonality in equipment. The first locomotives in America for use on railroads were imported from England. In the case of the Delaware & Hudson Canal Company, and many of the roads from the 1830s, the railroad was built to accommodate the locomotives. At least one of the early British railways adjusted its gauge after building the railway, widening it by a half-inch to reduce the binding between the rails and the wheels. In America, the first railroad (the granite railroad in Quincy) was

RIGHT

This remarkable view of Martinsburg, West Virginia, in 1858, shows the yards packed with "Camels." Designed by Ross Winans of the Baltimore & Ohio, these were the first coal-burning locomotives to be produced in large numbers. Nearly 300 were built and some ran for more than forty years. The cab was placed atop the boiler to reduce the weight on the firebox. The circular tubs in the foreground are loaded with coal bound for Baltimore.
Baltimore & Ohio Railroad photo, MARS

built to five-foot gauge. The Stourbridge Lion was built to four-foot three-inch gauge. Cooper's little engine on the Baltimore & Ohio Railroad Company was four-foot six-inch gauge and the Mohawk & Hudson was four-foot nine-inch gauge, as was the Pennsylvania Railroad predecessor Philadelphia & Columbia. Roads such as the Erie and the predecessors of the Lackawanna Railroad were built to six-foot gauge. The four-foot eight and one-half inches Central of New Jersey carried the six-foot gauge Lackawanna to Tidewater by laying a third rail. The Morris & Essex in the 1830s was a four-foot ten-inch road that changed to six-foot after being purchased by the Lackawanna, which later

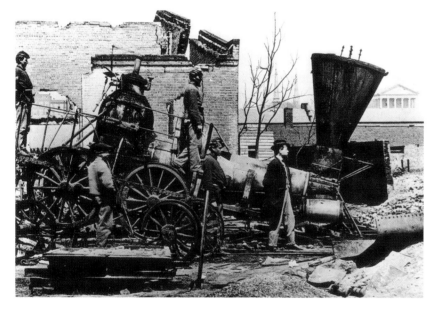

ABOVE
The Civil War was hell on the railroads, especially those in the South. Here we see some of the carnage in 1865 down at the depot in Richmond after the fall of the capital of the Confederacy. The American Civil War was the first war in which railroads played an important strategic role.
Library of Congress, MARS

converted the entire system to four-foot eight and one-half inches in one day. Other oddities included the Camden & Amboy at four-foot nine and three-quarter inches and the Baltimore & Susquehanna at four-foot nine and one-quarter inches.

However, in the northeast most roads were building to a gauge of four-foot eight and one-half inches, as were many iron roads in Maine, Massachusetts and Connecticut. But the railroads in the south preferred a five-foot gauge, and the Erie convinced the Ohio & Mississippi (which became part of the Baltimore & Ohio Railroad Company) to build to six foot—which meant that there were six-foot gauge railway connections between New York and St. Louis via Chicago. Also bucking the trend in

gauge was a network of railroads constructed in rural Maine toward the end of the 1870s; here, two foot was all there was between the rails (a two-foot gauge was first used in Massachusetts, however.)

The question of gauge was not just a mechanical one: it also became a matter of political concern. When Congress was drafting the Pacific Railroad Act in the early 1860s, and the Union Pacific Railroad was being formed under government auspices, the President was requested to specify the track gauge. The Southern states were lobbying heavily for the first transcontinental railway to take a southerly route, while the North wanted a northerly path. Abraham Lincoln carefully considered the issue of gauge (though the debate about the route could have delayed the passing of the Pacific Railroad Act for many years). He chose a five-foot gauge to match the roads in the South. As an attorney in Springfield, Missouri, Lincoln had acted for Illinois Central on occasion, which meant that he was already familiar with both gauges.

All of this meant that, by the time of America's centennial in 1876, nearly two dozen different track gauges were in use coast to coast, from the Maine two-footers mentioned above to a log-railed logging line in Oregon with eight foot between the timbers. Roads such as the New York Central had different gauges on some of its subsidiary railroads, and it had specially equipped cars with extra-wide tires that could roll on different gauges. (A few derailments with numerous fatalities on such equipment showed that such "adjustable trucks" were not the best solution to the problem.)

Often, railroads with a gauge anywhere near five foot called its own gauge "standard." Most roads had to simply transload freight between the cars of its interchange partners, and a few companies actually swapped the trucks on incoming cars from another road, and swapped them back again when the car was heading off-line. Illinois Central would actually change the trucks on its passenger trains that moved between gauges (Illinois Central was standard north of Cairo, Illinois, and five-foot

gauge south of it). The Grand Trunk Railway had some freight cars with telescoping axles that could be manually adjusted to varying gauges.

The Civil War was significant to America's railroads; it was, after all, the first war in which railroads played a key role. The trains carried troops, supplies, armaments, and mail. The war proved, more than any other single event, that the railroads needed to be able to roll cars freely and without delay over each other's tracks. It became clear that a common gauge was needed.

The politics surrounding the war were also important to the development of the industry in other ways. As the Southern states seceded from the Union, its members of Congress left, too. The

Pacific Railroad Act was thus passed with Yankee influence all over it. The first transcontinental railroad would take a northerly route, and it would be built to the standard gauge of four foot eight and one-half inches used by the politically powerful railroads in the East. By this time, standard gauge (as referring to four foot eight and one-half inches) was part of the lexicon. After the war, many railroads in the south that needed rebuilding did so to standard gauge. Among the last of the standard gauge holdouts was the Illinois Central, which converted the southern broad gauge portions of its system during August 1881, followed by the Mobile & Ohio in 1885. On February 2, 1886, a convention of Dixie railroad presidents agreed to make the complete change by June 1 of that year. The last road to change was the Louisville & Nashville which—seemingly defiant of the North—narrowed its track to four foot nine inches. Louisville & Nashville finally went standard in the 1890s.

While the Roman chariots and the ruts in the Appian Way may have had a slight influence on

railroad gauge, the term "standard" as referring to four foot eight and one-half inches is not as recent as the Civil War. But what if the Southern roads, Abraham Lincoln, and the Erie had been right in trying to establish a broader gauge universally? Railroad cars riding on wheels five- or six-foot apart could be eleven- or twelve-foot wide, rather than today's ten-foot width. A wider freight car would carry a much greater volume of goods, thus giving today's railroads an even greater advantage over other forms of transportation. And commuter cars would be capable of handling many more people, while long-distance train travelers would have more room in the diner and in the sleeper.

STANDARD TIME

Today, the entire world sets it clocks according to time zones. But the system of time zones was not the clever act of the world's congress—it was born from the frustration of railroaders trying to keep a schedule. Even after the American Civil War, humankind was keeping "sun time," or more commonly "local time." When the sun was straight up, it was noon. Sundials were not unusual. Each town had a "regulator" clock, and the gentlemen would visit this regulator to set their pocket watches. From the pocket watch, the clock on the wall at home could be set. If that town had a railroad, quite often that town's "regulator" was hanging on the wall in the station agent's office. Of course, it was not that each town literally kept its own time; but nearby towns often grouped together to create, in effect,

micro time zones. Nationally, the consequences were chaotic: contemporary accounts list Wisconsin as having thirty-eight local times, Michigan with twenty-seven and Indiana with twenty-three. How did the railroads operate under these circumstances? Most picked a terminal and scheduled to that, but sprawling Union Pacific (for example) operated by at least six different clocks. The passenger station in Buffalo was well known for having three clocks, one for each of the three tenant railroads. Unsurprisingly, by the 1870s American railroads had begun a move to standardize schedules and timekeeping. Not much came of this effort.

However, in St. Louis in October 1883, railroad timekeepers and the American Railway Association finally agreed that from Sunday, November 18, 1883, all railroad clocks would keep to four time zones across the country. But making such a change was not that simple. Contemporary newspapers reported opposition by some people, who thought the new system was "contrary to nature." This was not mere stubbornness: it was an era when the railroads were seen by many as having a "public be damned" attitude, not least because of their price

wheels. Predictably, curves in the track were a common cause of derailments.

Isaac Dripps, a self-taught mechanic on the Camden & Amboy, New Jersey's first railroad, devised the first locomotive "pilot," a single set of wheels in front of the driving wheels that help to guide the locomotive into curves. But in the process, he disconnected the lead pair of drivers and loosened them better to steer into the curves. Dripps converted what was built as an 0-4-0 into a 4-2-0. The locomotive—the John Bull—had been built by Stephenson in Newcastle, England and bought by Stevens of Hoboken. Dripps assembled this locomotive without instructions or drawings in 1831. Dripps' pilot soon evolved into a giant wooden wedge to shoo livestock from the track. The cow-catcher was born.

In addition to being New Jersey's first locomotive with the first cow-catcher, the John Bull had a horizontal boiler that burned wood, and it was soon equipped with a headlight and bell, plus a cab to protect the crew. It was the first locomotive to contain all of the details that years later were considered to make a locomotive distinctly American. (While replicas of many early engines exist, the original Stephenson-built John Bull rests in the Smithsonian Institution, and it was fired up and run for the 150th anniversary of the first day it ran in America, September 15, 1981. The Bull ran with a muffled but distinct and loud chuff, much like locomotives built 100 years later. It was a smooth runner that pulled its coach with ease, just as Stephenson promised it would in 1831.) It was successful enough in 1831 for the Camden & Amboy to build fifteen copies. From the John Bull evolved larger locomotives of varied wheel arrangements. Dripps and Stevens designed and built an 0-8-0 and a 6-2-0; both were larger than the John Bull. Ross Winans of the Baltimore & Ohio, meanwhile, pioneered many ideas, including the 2-8-0 "Camel," distinctive for its engineer's cab mounted

gouging. One popular response to the railroads' proposal was, "I keep God's time, not that of the railroads."

So great was the opposition that the US Attorney General declared that government offices had no right to change timekeeping until directed to do so by Congress. As private enterprises, the railroads did not require an Act of Congress to make the change—so they proceeded with it. Newspapers referred to the day of implementation (November 18) as "the day of two noons:" railroad employees had to obtain the time of the "new" noon, then re-set their watches, and re-start work, when it arrived. Along the Pennsylvania Railroad, for example, a telegrapher's key was connected with the pendulum of the clock at the observatory in Allegheny, Pennsylvania. When the dispatcher's clock struck noon, the pendulum was stopped. It was restarted again at noon standard time which was calculated according to the meridian.

Many people continued to object to keeping railroad time; but if they wanted to ride a train, they had to be there when the trains were. And so standard time was eventually adopted by everyone, and Congress formally adopted railroad time in 1918.

LOCOMOTIVE DEVELOPMENT

Locomotives and rolling stock also improved with time. Early locomotives such as the Stourbridge Lion, Cooper's Tom Thumb, and the Best Friend of Charleston were all four-wheeled carts. The locomotive's entire weight rested on those four

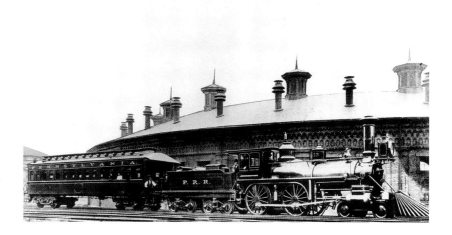

high over the boiler and above the driving wheels.

New locomotive ideas and locomotive builders flourished. By the 1840s and 1850s, the most common and versatile locomotive in America was the 4-4-0. The Whyte system of wheel arrangements and type-names did not come into use until 1901; Whyte deemed the 4-4-0 as the American-type. Meanwhile, a Philadelphia watchmaker named Baldwin began building locomotives, and the New Jersey city of Paterson was growing into the largest builder of locomotives in the world, with five competing factories. During the Civil War, 4-4-0 was the most common wheel arrangement in use. For freight service, the 4-4-0 led to the development of the 2-6-0, which led to the 2-8-0. Larger wheels enable a locomotive to travel further with each cylinder stroke, and such became desirable for passenger service where speed was important. In passenger service, the 4-4-0 led to the 4-6-0, and eventually to the 4-6-2. Locomotive development was still on the rise by the 1890s, but designers never did fully understand the expansive power of steam until the next century.

THE BRAKES

Being able to stop a train is, perhaps, more important than being able to start it. When railroading began, equipment had minimal braking apparatus, and quite often the mules were run over by the very wagon they were hauling. From the 1830s, the brakes on equipment were crude inventions that worked simply by applying a drag to the tread of one or more wheels. As the equipment grew in size, more elaborate systems were developed, most of which were activated by the turning of a brake wheel that pulled a chain that tightened the brake shoes against the wheel tread. Most brake wheels were located on the roof of freight cars, and on the end platforms of passenger cars. Brakemen had to ride the tops of the freight cars, and they would apply the brakes after hearing a whistle command from the engineer. During these early days of railroading, freight trains traveled, usually, in the area of ten to twenty mph. Brakemen carried hardwood clubs, usually of hickory, that could be wedged into the spokes of a brake wheel to help gain more torque in applying and releasing brakes. The typical brakeman was responsible for four to five cars each. A twenty-five-car freight train would have five men riding the car tops. These same five men would assist in switching by standing on the ground helping to relay hand signals around curves. A brakeman's job on the railroad was perhaps the most dangerous in the world. The tops of early freight cars were not designed or equipped, really, to carry a rider. When the weather was bad or cold, a seat on a boxcar roof was not comfortable. And the brakeman had to jump between cars to get to all five assigned to him, regardless of rain, sleet or snow. Quite often, a train would arrive with fewer brakemen than it had left with. It was perilous work, indeed.

Then, in 1869, George Westinghouse patented a practical air brake, a device that could apply or

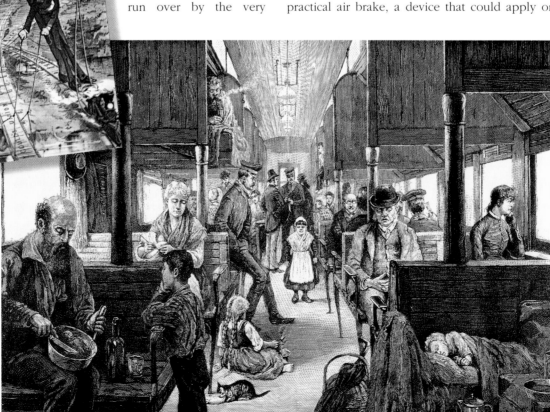

release the brakes on a train with the use of air compressed by pumps on the steam locomotive. An air reservoir and three-way control valve on each freight car controlled the application or release of the brake. But this system seemed expensive at the time, and the railroads were reluctant to spend the money. However, once they complied, the railroads were able to haul more cars in longer freight trains. The higher revenue from the longer trains more than offset the cost of the brakes. Today, Westinghouse Air Brake Company (WABCO) remains a leader in the field, and its air brake system is based on the same basic principles as before. However, back in the 1870s when the air brake systems were being installed, the locomotive engineers' union had threatened to strike—they didn't feel it was their job to stop the train, too.

THE TRANSCONTINENTAL RAILROAD

No event in railroading was as important to the growth of America as the joining of East and West at Promontory Summit on May 10, 1869. When the spike maul struck that final blow, the five-month journey across America (or down and around the tip of South America, by ship) was reduced to a matter of days. Humans are naturally intrigued by any new frontier. In the 1830s, when railroading was blossoming, anywhere west of the Mississippi River was regarded as the Frontier. Though populated with Native Americans, the West offered new opportunities for those willing to take the chance. It was the "manifest destiny" of the United States to expand the country's borders to both coasts. After the victory in the war with Mexico in 1848, treaties opened up the West by

ceding California to the United States. But it was the discovery of gold at Sutter's Mill in the Sierra Nevada foothills that really got Americans heading West. The westward movement toward California gold was among the largest migrations of people in American history.

The Pacific Railroad Act of 1862 passed quickly through the Congress, partially because by this time the South had seceded and the Civil War was in full swing. Building the transcontinental railroad had become a national emergency, to reach the riches of the West, to bind California to the Union, and to attract conscripts for military duty. The 1862 act called for the formation of the Union Pacific Railroad, which would build west from Omaha, and it authorized the privately held Central Pacific to build east from Sacramento. Both railroads were building on federal lands and were granted large

sections of land along the right of way. In addition, both companies raised construction capital through US bonds for each mile of track built. The bonds were, in fact, a loan to be repaid at 6 per cent interest within thirty years, though the railroads were required to be completed in twelve years.

By June 1863, ground had been broken in Sacramento. In less than six years, on May 10, 1869, the two railroads met at Promontory, Utah. Building nearly 2000 miles of railroad, some of it over the most rugged mountain passes, was truly one of man's greatest engineering feats. Today, the Southern Pacific (successor to the Central Pacific) has been merged into the very same Union Pacific that was present at Promontory. But much of the railroad's route has changed little from the original alignment built in the 1860s.

PART 2 TWO

THE GOLDEN AGE & BEYOND

The industrial revolution was in full swing during the 1880s. Industrial giants such as Carnegie made steel available and the railroads brought it to where it was needed. By the time of World War I, however, the railroads were a little worn out, and the government formed the United States Railroad Administration (USRA) to manage the entire network, designing new freight cars and locomotives.

The decade of the 1920s was significant. This was when designers finally understood the principles of steam locomotives to create what was called "Super Power;" it was also when the first diesel engine was tried in a locomotive in America. In the 1930s, streamliners were all the rage, and both locomotive types were streamlined in an effort to keep passengers on the rails, and off the roads.

By the end of World War II, the steam locomotive was tired. The more-efficient, lower-maintenance diesels were eclipsing the labor-intensive steam locomotive and, in 1960, the steam era ended.

The 1960s and 1970s will be remembered for the decline of the passenger train nationally but, by the 80s, the railroads were strong and competitive with trucking. The rails were luring international cross-country container traffic. Omens were good.

FROM THE SEA TO THE GREAT LAKES

The area encompassing New York, New Jersey, Pennsylvania and Ohio was the earliest region to benefit from railroading. At the heart of this region, in New York City, lies the modern American railroading engine: Wall Street. Railroad corporations sell stock and report the results to their shareholders. New Jersey and the area serving New York grew to become the area most densely traversed by railroads, and it's a distinction that remains to this day.

In addition to simply bringing riders into and out of New York, and the transportation of goods between New York and Philadelphia, railroads were built to haul coal from the anthracite fields of eastern Pennsylvania to city homes and offices. The anthracite roads also built a web of main and branch lines to reach the early iron mines of northern New Jersey. As the steel industry later grew on the banks of the Monongahela, the Allegheny and Ohio Rivers near Pittsburgh, Pennsylvania, railroads radiated from there to compete for the massive traffic a steel mill requires. Between New York and Pittsburgh lay the Alleghany and Pocono chains of the Appalachian Mountains, with defiles that brought out the best from civil and locomotive engineers in order to overcome these challenges.

LEFT

The vast Pennsylvania Railroad had a few branch lines that conveyed the charm of a much smaller company. The Elmira Branch connected the central Pennsylvania coal fields with Lake Ontario, and it was one of the last holdouts for PRR steam. One of Pennsy's ponderous I1sa-class 2-10-0s, numbered 4587, is heading south on September 1, 1956, with a string of empty coal hoppers returning to the mines. The operator at Kendall Tower south of Elmira is about to hoop up a train order to give the engineer authority to run on the next section of track.

Jim Shaughnessy

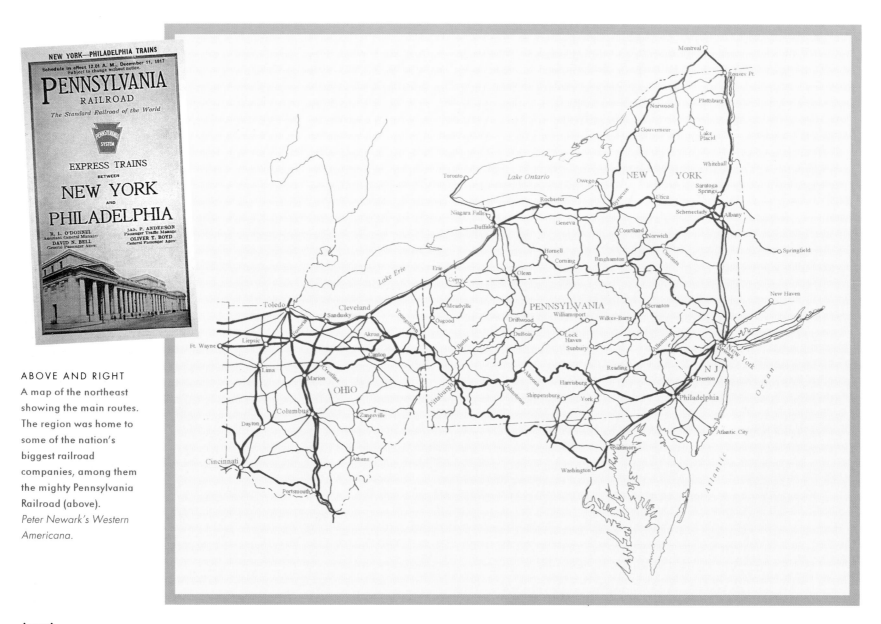

NEW YORK—PHILADELPHIA TRAINS

Schedule in effect 12.01 A. M., December 11, 1917
Subject to change without notice.

PENNSYLVANIA
RAILROAD
The Standard Railroad of the World

EXPRESS TRAINS
BETWEEN
NEW YORK
AND
PHILADELPHIA

R. L. O'DONNEL
Assistant General Manager
DAVID N. BELL
General Passenger Agent

JAS. P. ANDERSON
Passenger Traffic Manager
OLIVER T. BOYD
General Passenger Agent

ABOVE AND RIGHT
A map of the northeast
showing the main routes.
The region was home to
some of the nation's
biggest railroad
companies, among them
the mighty Pennsylvania
Railroad (above).
*Peter Newark's Western
Americana.*

THE HEART OF AMERICAN RAILROADING is in New York City. Wall Street, to be exact. Behind the pillars of the New York Stock Exchange (NYSE) lie the ghosts of every railroad dating back to the Delaware & Hudson Canal Company of the 1820s. It was here where financing was arranged, the stocks issued and traded and sold to generate sufficient capital to build the dream railroad of the day. Some raised enough; many did not. Literally hundreds of railroad companies were chartered: several never laid a stick of rail—but many did.

More than 150 years later, however, Wall Street is as big a part of the railroad industry as ever. Each quarter the chief executive officers (CEOs) and chief operating officers (COOs) stage elaborate meetings to present to Wall Street analysts the current results and rosy forecasts for

the next quarter. The smaller railroads may not rate the prestige of an NYSE stock listing, but the small stocks trade on Wall Street, too. The NYSE is so big that when it has a bad day, the entire world economy reflects it. And some of the biggest players on Wall Street are the Class 1 railroads.

Railroading began in the northeast. The first commercial railroads were built to haul goods to and from New York City—even the Delaware & Hudson Canal was conceived as a way to get anthracite there from Pennsylvania. By the 1840s railroads were radiating from Manhattan like tentacles from a squid. By the turn of the century, the roads were well established and the rail routes of 1900 aren't drastically different from today.

Eastward from New York ran the New York, New Haven & Hartford. To the north ran the New York Central (NYC), which had main lines on both

sides of the Hudson River; it turned west at Albany. Heading west from the New Jersey side of the Hudson River were the Pennsylvania, the Central of New Jersey (CNJ), the Lehigh Valley, the Lackawanna, the New York, Susquehanna & Western and the Erie. The struggling New York, Ontario & Western came south from the Catskill and the Shawungunk mountains upstate using the NYC tracks along the Hudson River's west bank.

The CNJ stretched from the Hudson to the anthracite fields of northeastern Pennsylvania. It did well early on, but foundered financially— literally spending more years in receivership and bankruptcy than it did in solvency. The Lackawanna and Lehigh Valley railroads got as far west as Buffalo, and both had to rely on connections with other roads to reach Chicago. The New York Central, the Pennsylvania and the

PRINCIPAL OPERATORS

Baltimore & Ohio (CSX)

Central Railroad of New Jersey (CR)
Delaware & Hudson
Delaware, Lackawanna & Western (CR)
Erie (CR)
Lehigh Valley (CR)

New York Central (CR)
New York, Chicago & St. Louis
(Nickel Plate Road) (NS)
New York, Ontario & Western
New York, Susquehanna & Western

Pennsylvania Railroad (CR)

Reading (CR)

CONTEMPORARY OPERATORS

Amtrak
Conrail
CSX Transportation
New York, Susquehanna & Western
Norfolk Southern Corporation
Canadian Pacific Railway
NJ Transit

(MODERN MERGED IDENTITIES ARE IN PARENTHESES)

RIGHT
The elevated railway era began in Manhattan in 1876 to ease New York City's overpopulation problem. This photo from the 1890s shows a steam-powered elevated train along 3rd Avenue. The five-cent fare was not increased until 1946 when the subways were replacing the elevateds.
TRH Pictures collection

Erie competed fiercely for the New York to Chicago trade.

Hosts of smaller regional railroads with fortunes tied to anthracite were also quite profitable throughout most of the 1900s. The Reading, the Lehigh & New England and the Delaware & Hudson, in addition to the CNJ and the Lackawanna, made a good living in the coal fields. These companies became known as the "anthracite roads." One of these, the Lackawanna, invented a fair maiden whose "gown stayed white, from morn 'til night, upon the Road of Anthracite" —before World War I, Phoebe Snow was one of the most famous fictional women in America.

The northeast was home to all of the major locomotive builders. In the nineteenth century, Paterson, New Jersey, was the locomotive capital of the world, with five renowned builders in the downtown district. Best known of the Paterson firms was the Rogers Locomotive Works. The General of American Civil War fame was a Rogers' engine, as was Central Pacific's Jupiter at the "golden spike ceremony," at Promontory, Utah.

By the twentieth century, the key locomotive builders were Baldwin near Philadelphia, the American Locomotive Works (Alco) near Albany, and the Lima Locomotive works in Lima, Ohio. When diesels vanquished steam, the major builders were Alco, Baldwin, General Electric in Erie, Pennsylvania, and Electro-Motive Corporation of Cleveland, Ohio—which at first was building locomotives at GE's Erie factory. Before World War II, General Motors would purchase EMC and they would build a new plant outside Chicago.

After the boom years of World War II and the decline of passenger services, corporate consolidations were inevitable. First, the New York, Ontario & Western called it quits in 1957, soon followed by the Lehigh & New England in 1962, its operations in Pennsylvania picked up by the CNJ. The first of the major mergers combined the Lackawanna and the Erie in 1960. After many years of looking for merger partners, the mighty New York Central merged with the giant Pennsylvania Railroad in 1968. Both roads had been teetering on bankruptcy and saw the consolidation as an opportunity for cost-cutting. The resulting Penn Central was the largest railroad system in America. The following year, bankrupt New Haven was added to Penn Central. Yet on June 21, 1970, the immense Penn Central filed for bankruptcy protection. It was the largest corporate bankruptcy in American history, the significance of which cannot be understated. Since the court was authorizing the payment of Penn Central's bills, it delayed the valuable interline payments owed to other railroads, causing the collapse of the entire northeast railroad system.

Motivated by the rest of the industry, the US Government formed Conrail, which began operations on April 1, 1976. To maintain rail competition, the Delaware & Hudson remained independent and was granted trackage rights over much of the system. Conrail combined all of the bankrupt eastern railroads and commuter services into a huge bankrupt railroad system: 17,000 route miles serving fourteen states. It foundered at first, but in 1981 Conrail hired Southern Railway's retired CEO L. Stanley Crane, who turned the railroad into one of the industry's great success stories. When the government privatized Conrail, it was the largest public stock offering in history.

Northeastern railroading in the 1990s was vibrant and profitable. Lines cast off by Conrail bred a host of colorful short lines with interesting motive power. The states of New Jersey, New York and Pennsylvania have financed commuter rail systems that rival those anywhere in the world. Amtrak's Northeast Direct service along the northeast corridor is running trains at 125mph and is the nation's state-of-the-art in track structure. It is also Amtrak's most profitable business center.

This view of the grand railroad station at Harrisburg, Pennsylvania, was made in the 1860s, just after the American Civil War. Shown here are four trains of the Pennsylvania, the Cumberland Valley, the Northern Central and the Philadelphia & Reading railroads. The Cumberland Valley and the Northern Central would later become part of the sprawling PRR system. Just a few years earlier, General Lee's Confederate armies were en route to Harrisburg when they encountered the Union troops at a small crossroads town called Gettysburg, about thirty-five miles to the south.
AAR photo, MARS

New York Central Railroad's 20th Century Limited was a brand new train when, in 1902, this photo was taken of the westbound train skirting the shores of Lake Erie in Ohio on Lake Shore & Michigan Southern tracks. With an all-Pullman consist the train was a worthy successor to NYC's Empire State Express of an earlier era.
Salamander Picture Library

RIGHT
Building a locomotive was literally all in two day's work at the Altoona Shops of the Pennsylvania Railroad. This series of views shows the progress of a typical 4-4-0, road number 1212 of the class of 1888. The PRR would build locomotives in its Altoona Shops, in addition to purchasing from nearby Baldwin Locomotive Works in Philadelphia. Altoona's engineers were among the first truly to understand steam design, and it produced some of the most successful designs of that wheel arrangement on any railroad. PRR's E6-class 4-4-2s, K4-class 4-6-2s and M1-class 4-8-2s are three examples.
Peter Newark's Western Americana

IN STEAM READY FOR TRIAL.
Tuesday, 2:50 p. m

16 HOURS 50 MINUTES WORK.

WHEELS UNDER AND CAB IN POSITION.
Tuesday, 7 o'clock a. m.

10 HOURS WORK.

BOILER IN POSITION.
Monday, Noon.

5 HOURS WORK.

ABOVE AND LEFT
Pennsylvania Station in New York City was a grand structure, comparable only to New York Central's Grand Central Terminal uptown. The grand concourse at Penn Station was one of the largest enclosed spaces when completed in 1910, and skylights allowed soft, natural lighting. The contemporary postcard shows the exterior of Penn Station, which was entirely funded by the railroad. The PRR was the first to tunnel under the Hudson River, giving its trains from the west direct access to midtown Manhattan; its competitors had to ferry passengers across the Hudson from New Jersey. *MARS*

BELOW
Grand Central Terminal, completed in 1913, was a masterpiece of its day and the pride of the New York Central. By placing all fifty-seven terminal tracks underground, the air rights above the terminal became some of the most prestigious real estate in Manhattan, supporting buildings such as the Waldorf Astoria. *MARS*

LEFT
The Baltimore & Ohio used ponderous articulated locomotives, primarily as pushers over its steep Sand Patch grade in southwestern Pennsylvania. One such example is 2-8-8-0 No. 7121, called a Mallet after French designer Anatole Mallet first designed a locomotive with a swiveling frame to negotiate curves.
B&O Museum, MARS

BELOW
Accidents do happen, and one occurred on the Cleveland, Cincinnati, Chicago & St. Louis Railroad on May 1, 1913, near Middletown, Ohio. Note how the wooden baggage car behind the locomotive was heavily damaged, a tendency that helped hasten the invention of steel railroad passenger cars.
Tom Kelcec collection

LEFT
When it built the Grand Central Terminal in 1910, New York Central also electrified its four-track main line to Croton Harmon, New York. Long distance trains left New York City pulled by electrics, which were swapped for steam at Croton. Note the elevated third rail near the track.
New York Central photo, MARS

The Pennsylvania Railroad made great use of 11-class 2-10-0s. These decapods were among the largest of that wheel arrangement on any road, and the PRR used them primarily on local and road freights, and as pushers on some mountain grades. In this scene, a new-looking 4471 was fully animated as it rolled past the camera without a train. The PRR owned 598 of these Decapods.
Peter Newark's American Pictures

The Delaware, Lackawanna & Western Railroad was born in 1851 in the northeastern Pennsylvania coal fields. It was best known at the turn of the century for hauling anthracite. Lackawanna also burned it in locomotives, but the fireboxes were too wide to accommodate the cab, so the engineer's perch was moved forward. The 970, at Hoboken, circa 1910, was one of these "Mother Hubbard," or "Camelback" types.
Photo by William B. Barry, Jr., collection of Ron Ziel

This 1925 view of the observation lounge car of the 20th Century Limited at Grand Central Terminal in New York City shows how attendents would handle the luggage of the first class passengers. Service was a hallmark of the 20th Century, and during the streamliner years a red carpet was actually laid on the platform to underscore the importance of the passenger. While the schedule catered to the business traveler, the posh accommodation appealed to the celebrities as well.
Peter Newark's American Pictures

The most luxurious and best-promoted train on the Pennsylvania Railroad was the Broadway Limited, named for PRR's well-maintained four-track main line, "the broad way". Its only rival for the lucrative New York-to-Chicago business traveler was the 20th Century Limited of the New York Central. This publicity photo shows the Broadway circa 1930 before the era of streamlining and air-conditioned coaches. The K4s 4-6-2s, a very successful design, handled this train until the end of steam, and some were streamlined to haul PRR's matching "fleet of modernism."
PRR photo, William Krattville collection

The Blue Comet was a luxury express train which connected Jersey City with the resort town of Atlantic City. It was discontinued in 1943. Despite this blue-and-cream color scheme, most trains were dark green.
Peter Newark's American Pictures

ABOVE
The Pennsylvania Railroad hired industrial designer Raymond Loewy to streamline locomotives and passenger cars for the Broadway Limited. Beneath the stylish lines and shrouding is K4s 4-6-2 No.3768, shown here near Philadelphia in 1937 soon after the locomotive was debuted and before the new cars had arrived. The unstreamlined 5358 opposite is the sister locomotive to 3768.
PRR photo, William Kratville collection

RIGHT
During the pre-World War II streamline era, the New York Central ordered ten class J3a Hudson-type steam locomotives with decorative shrouding for its 20th Century Limited. Industrial designer Henry Dreyfuss did the styling, and these locomotives later became an icon of American railroading. This is No.5445, the first of these Dreyfuss 4-6-4s, in March 1938 at the American Locomotive Company factory in Schenectady, New York.
New York Central Railroad, MARS

Pennsylvania's shark-nosed T1-class 4-4-4-4s were also streamlined by Raymond Loewy. Eighty of these unique duplex-drive locomotives were built by Baldwin in Philadelphia and at PRR's Altoona shops. They represent PRR's loyalty to the steam locomotive in an era when the diesel was proving itself. This 5526 was built at Altoona in 1942.
Baldwin photo, Salamander Picture Library

Raymond Loewy was also hired by PRR to design a carbody for the GG1 electric locomotive. Two of them are seen here in Washington, D.C., on April 8, 1960, at the Ivy City engine terminal just north of Union Station. These 6000hp locomotives were among the most successful electrics ever designed, and they lasted just under fifty years in service.
Jim Shaughnessy

RIGHT
Cleaning up after a wreck can be time-consuming work. Witness two steam cranes digging a locomotive and its tender out of the ballast among the mangled trackage and bent equipment. This wreck occurred on the Erie Railroad in Paterson, New Jersey, during the late-1930s when the westbound Lake Cities out of Jersey City derailed, causing no serious injuries. Delays due to this wreck were minimal, as trains were rerouted over Erie's parallel Bergen County Line.
Erie photo, Frank Quin and Ron Ziel collection

LEFT
Scranton, Pennsylvania, was the heart of the Lackawanna Railroad and the road's biggest shops. This typical 1940s scene shows trains gathered around the turntable at "hogtown," so named for all the helper locomotives—"hogs" to railroaders—kept here between assignments. Lackawanna's main back shops and turntable are to the left, out of view.
Railroad Avenue Enterprises collection

RIGHT
Streamlining began in the 1930s with the effort to lure passengers from colorful automobiles and back onto trains. The first true streamliner in the East was the B&O's Royal Blue that ran between New York City and the nation's capital city. Shown crossing the famous Thomas Viaduct near Baltimore in the 1930s, the Royal Blue traveled Reading and Jersey Central rails to reach Jersey City. The 4-6-2 locomotive and passenger car styling was created by Otto Kuhler, one of the best-known industrial designers of that era.

LEFT
Sodus Point, on Lake Ontario, was the northernmost terminus of the Pennsylvania's Elmira Branch. On July 4, 1956, this 2-10-0 is shoving six loaded coal hoppers up the incline of the pier to be dropped into the boat. Within a year diesels would be doing this work.
Jim Shaughnessy

RIGHT
Watkins Glen was located at the south end of Seneca Lake, one of New York's "five finger" lakes. The engineer of a southbound empty coal train was picking up orders from the block operator there on August 20, 1956. Female operators were unusual during this era.
Jim Shaughnessy

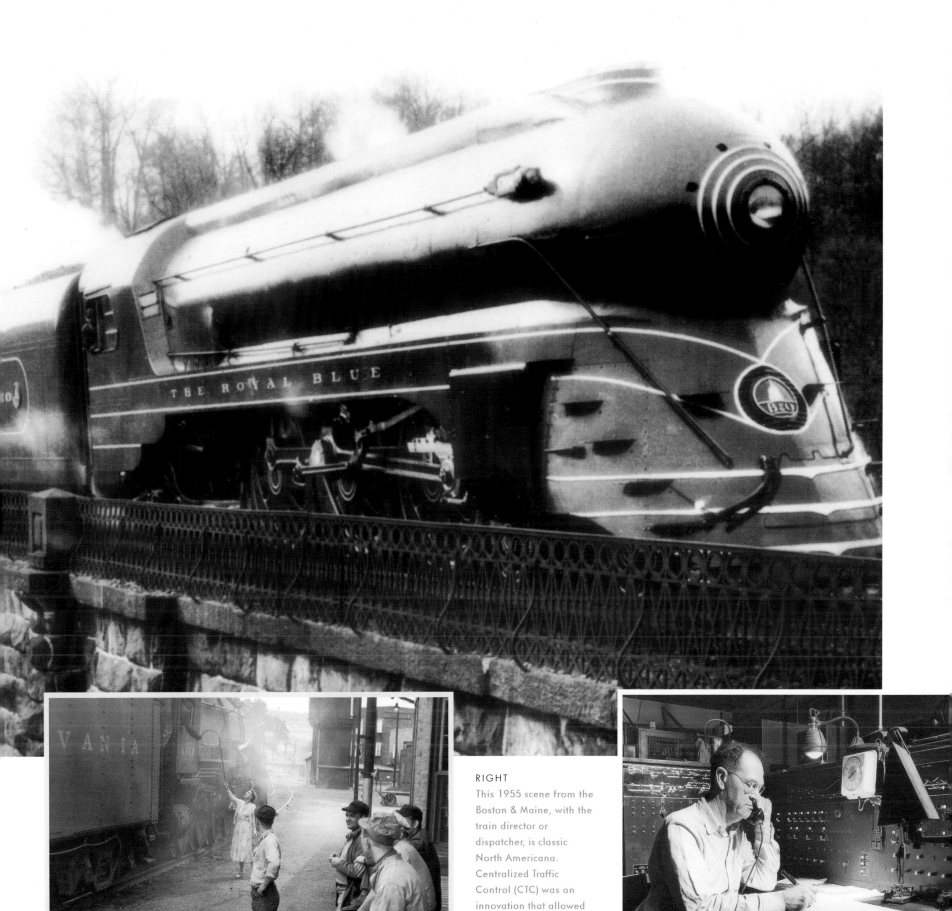

RIGHT
This 1955 scene from the Boston & Maine, with the train director or dispatcher, is classic North Americana. Centralized Traffic Control (CTC) was an innovation that allowed a dispatcher to control and monitor trains running in any direction on any track.
Jim Shaughnessy

RIGHT

The New York, Ontario & Western was a 541-mile regional railroad that connected Lake Ontario with New York City, though it used the tracks of New York Central's West Shore from Cornwall south to Weehawken, New Jersey. It also had a main line leg that extended to the anthracite fields in Scranton, Pennsylvania. It served primarily rural communities, and it struggled through most of its history. It dieselized early, but that only prolonged the inevitable. In May 1957, two months after this daily train was passing the Ontario & Western headquarters building in Middletown, New York, it was the first of the major railroads to be sold for scrap.
Jim Shaughnessy

LEFT

The Nickel Plate Road moved freight fast. With a fleet of Lima-built 2-8-4s, the Nickel Plate Road got freight trains up to a mile a minute, and it did its best to keep them at that speed until that train was on another railroad. With 2,100 miles of track, the Nickel Plate, officially the New York, Chicago & St. Louis, connected St. Louis and Chicago to Buffalo, New York. Nickel Plate's Berkshire-types were legendary, and the 779 is noteworthy for being the last locomotive built by the Lima Locomotive Works in Ohio.
Jim Shaughnessy

LEFT AND ABOVE
The Baltimore & Ohio's deluxe all-coach diesel streamliner was The Columbian, Train No.25 westward and Train 26 eastbound. It operated between Chicago and Baltimore via

Washington, D.C. It was entirely air conditioned, and equipped with a dining car, lounge car and glass-topped Strata Dome Car, still a novelty in 1949.
Baltimore & Ohio Railroad, MARS

It's a cold January evening in 1960 as a New York Central yard crew takes good care of a carload of brand new Ford Thunderbirds at West Albany, New York. The diesel switcher is an S2 model manufactured by the Alco Locomotive Works in Schenectady, New York, just a few miles from where this photo was taken. New York Central was a big customer of the on-line builder, and the S2 was one of the best-liked switcher designs of the time. Crews praised its spacious cab, ability to handle rough track, and its quick response to the throttle.
Jim Shaughnessy

Albany Union Station during the 1960s offered quite a variety of exotic motive power from two railroads. In this August 1968 scene, we see the Delaware & Hudson's most prestigious train, The Laurentian, dropping off passengers from Montreal pulled by Alco PA No.18, one of four former-Santa Fe PAs owned by the D&H. E8s numbers 4041 and 4042 are staged with two New York City-bound trains waiting for Capitol-district riders. The baggage wagon between the trains is heaped high with mail and express, staples that brought it much more revenue than the farebox during this era.
Jim Shaughnessy

RIGHT

Warwick, New York, was the headquarters, main shops and classification yards for the Lehigh & Hudson River Railway. A bridge line that connected the anthracite railroads at Allentown with the New Haven, the Erie, New York, Ontario & Western and the New York Central, the Lehigh & Hudson River Railway dieselized with a fleet of Alco locomotives. Thirteen 1600hp road switchers were later complemented with nine 2000hp Century 420s. At the Warwick shops, C420s 21 and 23 were being serviced on June 9, 1972, for their next assignment.
Robert R. Bahrs

RIGHT

Lehigh Valley stretched from the Hudson River opposite New York City to Buffalo, New York, and it competed directly with the Lackawanna for freight traffic. The "Valley" used a variety of diesel models, but its most powerful was a fleet of seventeen 2750hp Century 628s built by Alco. On September 23, 1972, the 626 and 625 were changing crews in Richards Yard, the largest of three west of Easton, Pennsylvania.
Robert R. Bahrs

LEFT
Rupert, Pennsylvania, is a rural town along the Susquehanna River where the Lackawanna's Bloomsburg line and the Reading Company's Catawissa Branch pass and intersect. Though it was called a branch, the Catawissa was Reading's northwest corner that reached the vast New York Central system at Williamsport. After the Penn Central merger in 1968 eliminated NYC's need to reach Williamsport, the line was cut back to Rupert. The Rupert-based switch engine was EMD-powered Baldwin 2711. *Robert R. Bahrs.*

ABOVE
The Pocono Mountains of eastern Pennsylvania were a stone wall that had plagued the Lackawanna since the 1860s. Every train had to win a war with gravity to reach the top, and skillful train handling was required to keep from running away on the other side. An early morning battle was lost on October 13, 1973, when Chicago-bound ACX-99 stalled at Mount Pocono after one of its four 1500hp GP7s developed trouble. A 3600hp SD45 was brought south from Scranton as a helper. *Robert R. Bahrs*

ABOVE

As the last rays of sun bathe the New Jersey cut-off on October 19, 1975, a pair of 3600hp SD45s lead an Erie Lackawanna train toward the New York metropolitan area. The train is climbing slightly upgrade on the Lubber Run Fill, one of ten fills and numerous cuts completed in 1911 when the cut-off opened. The reflection of the train in the still waters of Lake Lackawanna are symbolic, since the lake was formed in the borrow pits left over from the railroad's construction.
Robert R. Bahrs

RIGHT

Roseville Tunnel was blasted out of solid rock in 1911 by the Lackawanna Railroad as part of its New Jersey cut-off. After sixty-five years this line became part of Conrail, which considered the line redundant. Conrail GP40 3089 leads one of the very last eastbound freight trains through the 1,040-foot bore on a frosty February morning in 1978. The State of New Jersey has purchased this stretch of track, however, with plans to run commuter trains over it.
Robert R. Bahrs

An eight-car multiple-unit electric train dashes through the snow with morning commuters at Morristown, New Jersey, during February 1984. These venerable cars entered service in 1931 on the Lackawanna Railroad between Hoboken and Dover, New Jersey. Famous inventor Thomas Edison was at the throttle for a portion of the first run. Just after World War II, 38,000 people rode this equipment to and from their jobs each day. Commuter agency NJ Transit retired the "Lackawanna m.u.s" in 1984 after fifty-three years of service.
Robert R. Bahrs

It was a frigid Sunday afternoon on November 15, 1987, when westbound NJ Transit Train 7855 silently sailed into the sunset in the New Jersey Meadows. The train is crossing the drawbridge at Portal, so named since it is the first landmark west of the portals of the Hudson River tunnels. This line is part of Amtrak's Northeast Corridor line that connects New York City and Washington, D.C. It is North America's busiest passenger rail corridor and is also NJ Transit's most heavily traveled line, carrying more than 37,000 daily riders.
Author photo

The Northeast Corridor was built by the Pennsylvania Railroad in the nineteenth century, and it was electrified in the 1930s for more efficient operation. Connecting Washington, D.C., with New York City, the Pennsylvania Railroad was the only one from the west to bore tunnels for direct access to midtown Manhattan, and it thus got the lion's share of New York City's passenger and express business. Amtrak today calls it the Northeast Direct service, and 7000hp AEM7s handle most of the trains, such as the 944 pulling a six-car westbound through Portal Interlocking.
Author photo

NEW ENGLAND

An industrial center since before the American Revolution, Boston and the surrounding area made early use of railroading. Indeed, the first iron rails in America were laid just south of Boston at a quarry in Quincy, Massachusetts. Four major railroads spread like a web throughout New England and Maine, and the main lines of these systems are mostly intact today. The New Haven's Shoreline is becoming a high-speed passenger route under Amtrak's leadership, and New York Central's Boston & Albany across the middle of Massachusetts still rolls the most freight tonnage in the region. But today, as in years past, New England is known for quaint towns and scenic beauty, rustic and rural settings. The rustic nature even endured on New England's rails, which continued running milk trains and wooden boxcars longer than most other regions.

Today, paper and intermodal containers dominate the main line freights, while numerous short lines continue the tradition of rustic railroading. It is interesting to think that the railroad heyday in this region may be yet to come, as Amtrak builds a super railroad along the Connecticut coast, and three major railroads connect New England with the rest of the country, and the world.

LEFT
Nickel Plate Road 2-8-4 759 storms southward across the White River between West Hartford and White River Junction, Vermont. The 759 was the star of the Steamtown collection when, during the later 1970s, it was leased by the High Iron Company for a series of steam excursions throughout the region. This scene was part of a two-day trip between Concord and Montpelier Junction, Vermont, over the Central Vermont Railway. The 759 today is part of the Steamtown National Historic Site at Scranton.
Jim Shaughnessy

NEW ENGLAND

America began in New England with the Pilgrim Fathers, so it is perhaps appropriate that the first railroad on the continent would be built less than thirty miles from Plymouth Rock. In 1827 a granite quarry in Quincy (southeast of Boston) built a three-mile railway laid with strap rail on wooden planks five foot apart. Horses pulled the wagons. Of course, the Delaware & Hudson, the Baltimore & Ohio and the South Carolina railroads were to follow. But the Boston area was no stranger to early railroading as iron roads grew like bean sprouts. By 1900 the railroads of New England were sorted into systems that would last into the 1960s.

The most sprawling was the New York, New Haven & Hartford. Formed in 1872 with the consolidation of the New York & New Haven and the Hartford & New Haven, it aggressively leased and purchased more than 200 component companies to make up what simply became known as the New Haven. Connecting New York City with Boston, and reaching almost any other town worth reaching within New England's three southern states, it operated more than 10,000 miles of track at its peak and employed more than 125,000 people. At one point it also controlled the Boston & Maine, the Maine Central, the New York, Ontario & Western, and the Rutland. The New Haven was a giant among rail giants in a part of the country that seemed too small to contain it. Indeed, the railroad got too big for the territory and was hit hard by the Great Depression, filing for its first bankruptcy in 1935. Some trimming of trackage and dieselization helped, but the New Haven was financially shaky until forced by the Government in 1968 to join Penn Central. New Haven's most colorful era was during the 1940s and 1950s under the leadership of Frederick C. Dumaine and the influence of stockbroker Patrick McGinnis. The latter would gain control in 1954 and his legacy is a distinctive paint scheme and company heralds from designs by Herbert Matter.

The Boston & Maine was also extensive, with main lines that stretched from Boston east to Albany, northeast to Lincoln, New Hampshire, and due north to Portland, Maine. It also had a north-south main line that connected Springfield,

Massachusetts, Wells River, Vermont, and Berlin, New Hampshire, and several branches. Boston & Maine's Hoosac Tunnel stretched four and three-quarter miles through the Berkshire Mountains. When built in 1875, it was the world's longest tunnel, and it is still in use.

The Maine Central originated at Portland, Maine, and it extends northeast to the border towns of Vanceboro and St. Stephen via Bangor,

and it ran eastward through New Hampshire to St. Johnsbury, Vermont. It was a rugged railroad that braved some of the continent's harshest winters.

The Boston & Albany was a subsidiary of New York Central, and it connected its namesake cities with a high-tonnage main line. Cresting the Berkshire Mountains, the Boston & Albany demanded the best in motive power. Indeed, the prototype 2-8-4 of Lima's famous Superpower

PRINCIPAL OPERATORS

Bangor & Aroostook

Boston & Maine (GTI)
Central Vermont (NECR)
Canadian Pacific Railway

Maine Central (GTI)
New York, New Haven & Hartford (CR)
New York Central (CR)

Rutland

CONTEMPORARY OPERATORS

Amtrak
Conrail
CSX Transportation
Guilford Transportation
New England Central
Norfolk Southern

(MODERN MERGED IDENTITIES ARE IN PARENTHESES)

RIGHT
An 1879 image of the Boston, Concord & Montreal Railroad's brand new 2-6-0 Mogul-type locomotive. The artist even included the buildings of the Manchester Locomotive Works which built it. *Peter Newark's Western Americana collection*

design was named for the Berkshires. Today, the Boston & Albany is still a major Conrail route.

The main lines moved the tonnage, but the regionals had the charm. The Rutland originated in Bellows Falls, Vermont, and ran north to the Canadian border at Rouses Point, and then west to Odgensburg, New York, along the St. Lawrence River. Headquartered in Rutland, Vermont, this line was arguably New England's most scenic.

The Bangor & Aroostook stretched north from the "downeast" coastal town of Searsport, north through Bangor to Fort Kent in northernmost Maine. Its diesel years are best remembered for the older units that stayed in service years longer than almost any other railroad in America.

The Central Vermont, owned by Canadian National, connected Montreal with New London, Connecticut, on Long Island Sound. Although a child of Canadian National, the Central Vermont had a mind and a look all its own; its motive power was all-American, but a little bit Canadian.

Beginning in 1968, when the nearly bankrupt New Haven and Penn Central joined, New England's railroading changed dramatically. The marriage didn't work, of course, and the partnership formed the nucleus of Conrail in 1976. Many branch lines were abandoned, while one—the Providence & Worcester, an original component road of the New Haven—brought itself back to life and continues to operate today.

In 1981 two financiers formed Guilford Transportation to buy the Maine Central and its Portland Terminal subsidiary. In 1983, Guilford bought the Boston & Maine, which included the tiny Springfield Terminal. In 1984, Guilford bought the Delaware & Hudson, which was Conrail's only competitor outside New England. Guilford merged all its lines into the Springfield Terminal. An unfortunate labor strike followed, causing the bankruptcy of the Delaware & Hudson, which was ultimately purchased by Canadian Pacific.

Throughout the 1990s changes continued. Conrail prospered. Springfield Terminal, now just the Boston & Maine and Maine Central, was building a steady paper trade. The Central Vermont was sold to Railtex subsidiary New England Central. The Rutland was partially abandoned, but large segments became the Vermont Railway and the Green Mountain Railway. Interestingly, these Rutland segments reunited in 1997 and are controlled by the Vermont Railway. Holding company IronRoad Railways purchased the Bangor & Aroostook, the International of Maine division from Canadian Pacific, plus a former Canadian Pacific branch into Newport, Vermont. IronRoad operates each as a separate company with historic or regional names. Emons Industries bought Canadian National's Grand Trunk Eastern subsidiary, resurrecting the historic St. Lawrence & Atlantic name. Branch line spin-offs have created many colorful short lines.

Amtrak dominates the region's passenger railroading, but it is cheering to know that one tourist line, the steam-powered Mount Washington Cog Railway, has operated every day since it began in 1869, except for brief halts during both the world wars. While New England railroading has changed, it certainly isn't dull.

LEFT
America's early railroaders continued the English tradition of naming locomotives. Once the telegraph became the standard method of dispatching trains and recording movements in the 1880s, the names were dropped to save the telegrapher time. The Hampstead, see here in 1880, was built for the Worcester, Nashua & Rochester Railroad.
MARS

ABOVE
During the 1800s the most common steam locomotive wheel arrangement was the 4-4-0 (four pilot wheels, four driving wheels, no trailing wheels). First built in America, the 4-4-0 became known as the American standard, or American-type, wheel arrangement. New England had 4-4-0s on all of its main and branch line railroads and Central Vermont 4-4-0 101 is a very typical locomotive of the 1880s.
Burlington Northern Railroad, MARS

The Rhode Island Locomotive Works is another of New England's numerous small manufacturers, and it turned out this trim little 4-4-0 for the Boston & Maine Railroad in 1871. It and its crew posed for a picture in 1899 at the Salem, Massachusetts, roundhouse. In this broadside view it is possible to see the workings of the Stephenson valve gear common during this era. The motion of the driving wheels operates levers between the frame which is transferred to the slide valve above the cylinders. This locomotive remained in service until 1908.
MARS

The Manchester (New Hampshire) Locomotive Works was one of many locomotive builders in New England. Fitchburg Railroad 4-4-0 No.31, shown circa 1900, was built by Manchester and the growing Boston & Maine Railroad had leased the Fitchburg in 1900, later renumbering this locomotive to 965. With no crew in the cab, the centered valve gear and the sparkling clean condition suggest that the 31 is either on display or posing for a company portrait. The Russia-iron boiler jacket color is common for the era.
MARS

ABOVE
Boston's South Station is one of the grand railroad depots of the United States. This 1905 postcard view shows the brand new structure in all its glory, with the elevated railway passing by in front. South Station is one of three major depots in Boston, and it served primarily the New Haven and New York Central passengers. The Boston & Maine railroad used North Station.
Peter Newark's American Pictures collection

RIGHT
This 1910 scene shows Boston & Maine No.525, and behind that baggage car are likely three or four wooden coaches supported by truss-rod underframes. World War I and improvements in the steel industry in just a few years would bring great changes in appearance and performance: steel passenger cars would replace wooden ones, while larger locomotives would be required to pull them.
MARS

ABOVE
Boston & Maine 4-4-0
No.53 is riding the
Charlestown,
Massachusetts, turntable
in this view made circa
1910. The coal heaped
high in the tender and the
clean clothes on the crew
suggest that the 53 has
just been serviced and is
ready for a day's run.
Charlestown's turntable
and engine facility served
the locomotives using
Boston's North Station.
MARS

RIGHT
An unusual wheel
arrangement in New
England was the 4-8-0,
known as the Twelve-
Wheeler. This example is
a Boston & Maine L-class,
simmering outside the
Rochester, New
Hampshire, roundhouse
in 1912. Twelve-Wheelers
were useful both for
freight and passenger
trains on light-duty
branch lines with
moderate curves.
MARS

Boston & Maine's 3001-class 2-10-2s were among the largest and most powerful locomotives to operate in New England. In this 1926 scene at B&M's Billerica, Massachusetts, shop facilities, the railroad is experimenting with improving the performance even further. A tender booster—a small steam engine that drives the tender wheels to help the locomotive start a heavy train—was installed on the 3028. Note the white-painted driving rods on the tender truck and the new steam pipes to feed the booster. *MARS*

Seen at Penacook, New Hampshire, during the early 1930s at the height of the Great Depression, express business remains brisk on this southbound local passenger train from White River Junction to Concord. Note the station agent with a loaded baggage wagon putting packages into the Railway Post Office car immediately behind the locomotive. Boston & Maine's C-21-d-class 4-6-0s were ideal for this type of service, with driving wheels large enough to permit enough speed to make up time. *MARS*

BELOW
The New Haven utilized a diverse fleet of electric locomotives to pull trains between New Haven, Connecticut, and New York City. Box cab 078, shown at New Haven in 1938, is an EF-2 model built by Baldwin-Westinghouse in 1912. Capable of 1336hp, thirty-nine of these were in service, some lasting into the 1960s and the Penn Central merger. So useful and reliable were they that New Haven crews nicknamed them "Jeeps," comparing them to the utility of the military vehicle.
Salamander Picture Library

RIGHT
One of New Haven's elegant 4-6-2s is chasing the afternoon sun as it wheels the Merchants Limited on its westbound journey between Boston and New York City. The New Haven boasted a well-maintained right-of-way that followed the Connecticut coast for much of its journey through that state.
Peter Newark's American Pictures

ABOVE

Boston & Maine's ten P4a-Class 4-6-2s were among the finest locomotives of that wheel arrangement ever built. The Lima (Ohio) Locomotive Works, regarded as the Rolls-Royce of steam builders, designed and built them in two batches in 1934 and 1937. So proud was the Boston & Maine of its Pacific-type locomotives, numbered from 3710 to 3719, that it sponsored a contest for area school children to name each of them. The 3712, the East Wind, is shown about to depart Boston's North Station with Train 15 to Portland, Maine, on Saturday June 24, 1939. *MARS*

ABOVE
Photography of railroad subjects during World War II was prohibited, though many buffs lensed a frame now and then without incident. Here we see Boston & Maine class 5-1-a 2-10-2 No.3005 leading a train to Rigby, Maine, to interchange with the Maine Central in 1942.
MARS

RIGHT
The Rutland Railroad had some quaint little hamlets with procedures to match. Witness this late-1940s scene at Mount Holly, Vermont: the operator will attach a flimsy paper train order to each of those hoops, which he will hand up to the passing engineer in the locomotive and conductor in the caboose to give that train authority to occupy the next section of track. By lighting that hanging kerosene lantern, the engineer will know to slow or stop for orders.
Jim Shaughnessy

LEFT
The distinctive blunt trucks from an Alco switcher dominate the foreground of this scene in the Portland Terminal roundhouse at Rigby Yard in South Portland, Maine. The Portland Terminal was a switching road, jointly owned by the Maine Central and the Boston & Maine, that served both railroads and the local customers. Alco switchers are fun to watch while these vocal machines handle their daily chores. Rigby was regarded as one of the last bastions of Alco motive power in the region. Guilford Transportation purchased both parent railroads in 1981, rendering the terminal unnecessary.
Jim Shaughnessy

RIGHT
Skiers were big business for the Boston & Maine, which kept track of snow totals at numerous resorts that were located near the railroad. Many railroads developed or invested in resort and recreation as a way to increase off-peak ridership. Union Pacific actually invented the ski lift for its resort in Idaho. The date is February 7, 1946, at North Station in Boston, and this returning war veteran is obviously not a skier, or he would be pointing at Rutand, Vermont, or Quebec, the only areas reporting a powder surface.
Boston & Maine, Salamander Picture Library

LEFT
Rural New England was dairy country, and the railroads during the steam era hauled the lion's share of the milk to creameries and markets. During August 1946, at Burlington, Vermont, the Rutland Railroad's Green Mountain Flyer is getting under way with six milk cars, a Railway Post Office car and two passenger cars in tow. Coupled to the tender of the 2-8-2 are insulated refrigerator cars to keep the ten-gallon milk cans cold, and modern milk tank cars that carry it in massive glass-lined tanks.
Jim Shaughnessy

ABOVE
The New Haven Trap Rock Company operated a six-mile railroad to haul stone from a quarry to a plant near Branford, Connecticut. It operated small steam locomotives in concert with small diesel-electrics. The 0-4-0t No.43 was one of the last two in service on the line, and is shown on July 14, 1956, spotting hopper cars at the screen house, where the gravel is sorted by size. Outbound "trap rock" was shipped in railcars or barges across Long Island Sound. Both tank engines were retired in 1960.
Jim Shaughnessy

RIGHT
Crawford Notch was
Maine Central's cross to
bear, as its heavy grades
tested the mettle of train
crews and locomotives
alike. It was Maine
Central's main line west
to reach Canadian Pacific.
Among the freight was
one passenger train in
each direction. On a
sunny Saturday, May 15,
1954, Train 163 was
rolling south across Wiley
Brook trestle bound for
Portland, having just
made its 3:53 p.m. stop
at the Crawford Notch
depot. While the
passenger counts may
have been low, this train
was still carrying a milk
car, a railway post office
car and a bulk mail
storage car ahead of
the coach.
Jim Shaughnessy

ABOVE

St. Albans, Vermont, hosted the main offices and shops of the Central Vermont Railway, owned by Canadian National. On April 11, 1955, the northbound Ambassador is making its 8:01 p.m. station stop at St. Albans, en route to Montreal. Canadian National 4-6-2 5291 is doing the honors this day; it's not unusual to see Canadian motive power pulling Central Vermont trains. The Ambassador connected Montreal with both Boston and New York City via the Boston & Maine and New Haven railroads, respectively.
Jim Shaughnessy

RIGHT

This Central Vermont Railway local freight was heading north toward Rouses Point as it met two St. Johnsbury & Lamoille County (St. J&LC) locomotives at Swanton, Vermont, on a summer day in the mid-1950s. The "St. J" switchers were waiting for freight cars in the CV train. The CV kept running steam for most of the 1950s, while the St. J&LC had dieselized early. In New England the kerosene indicator lamps on the switch machines are mounted higher in the air, so that they can be seen in deep snow.
Jim Shaughnessy

The steam era in America ended proudly on some railroads and almost unnoticed on others. All of the motion and apparent cacophony in this photograph, taken on April 22, 1956, at Haverhill, Massachusetts, proves that Boston & Maine 4-6-2 3713, named Constitution, went out with sound and fury and dignity. Boston & Maine ran a special Sunday train for railfans to commemorate the last run of steam. Designed and built by the Lima (Ohio) Locomotive Works, 3713 is now at Steamtown National Historic Site in Scranton, Pennsylvania, and is slated to be restored.
Jim Shaughnessy

LEFT
A boy and his dog watch a St. Johnsbury & Lamoille County mixed train climbing Clay Hill westbound out of St. Johnsbury, Vermont, in April 1955. Behind the locomotives are a milk tank car and a boxcar, typical pieces of rolling stock for New England.
Jim Shaughnessy

BELOW
Impressive is this April 1959 line-up of electric locomotives at the New Haven Railroad's Cedar Hill yard in its namesake Connecticut city. Electric locomotives are virtually pollution free, and New Haven's could collect power from either overhead catenary or through third rail pick-up shoes located near the wheels.
Jim Shaughnessy

ABOVE
The kerosene lantern lasted in railroading through the 1960s, completing a 100-year legacy that began with whale oil before the American Civil War. Railroad lanterns are distinguished from farmer's lanterns by the cage around the glass globe and the generous handle surrounding the chimney. With a properly trimmed wick, kerosene lamps could produce as much light as the modern battery lanterns today. Percy Fonda, a Boston & Maine dispatcher working at the tower in Fonda, N.Y., is adjusting the wick on his Dietz Vesta lantern on October 22, 1955.
Jim Shaughnessy

73

LEFT

The Rutland Railroad was a quaint and scenic Vermont regional line that captured the hearts of many train-watchers. Sadly, after a bitter labor strike, the Rutland opted for abandonment in 1961 but the state purchased it and leased viable segments to other operators. The Green Mountain Railroad operates between Rutland and Bellows Falls, keeping the feel of the old Rutland: this Falls-bound RS1 is crossing the bridge near Chester, Vermont, in 1983.
Don Ball collection

ABOVE

During the summer months the Boston & Maine (B&M) operated extra trains from Concord, New Hampshire, into the Lakes region of central New Hampshire. The extra trains during the 1950s and 1960s were actually self-propelled rail diesel cars from the Budd Company dubbed "Highliners." On Sunday August 27, 1961, a Highliner is picking up Boston-bound passengers at Weirs Beach along the Merideth Bay shores of Lake Winnipesaukee.
Jim Shaughnessy

ABOVE
Maine Central freight train RY-2 is rattling the windows in the Crawford Notch, New Hamsphire, depot as the four diesels labor loudly with a long train on June 19, 1966. This was the Maine Central's Mountain Division, which threaded trackage from Portland, Maine, through the White Mountains to reach the Canadian Pacific at St. Johnsbury, Vermont. Though this line was abandoned in the early 1980s with the Maine Central/Boston & Maine merger, it is operated today by the Conway Scenic Railroad.
Jim Shaugnessy

ABOVE

New Haven EP-5 No.371 leads a train through Bridgeport, Connecticut, during 1968, before New Haven became part of the giant Penn Central. New Haven owned ten of these distinctive rectifier electrics, which were known as "jets" among the railroaders. The EP5s were built by General Electric in 1954, and they were equipped to run on overhead catenary and third rail to enable operation into New York Central's Grand Central Terminal in New York.
Don Ball collection

RIGHT

Aroostook Valley Railroad forty-four-ton locomotives 12 and 11 are switching the Bangor & Aroostook (B&A) interchange at Presque Isle, Maine, on September 30, 1976. The Bangor & Aroostook locomotive can be seen in the distance, numbered 1776 and painted red-white-and-blue for the nation's bicentennial.
Mike Miterko

Providence & Worcester (P&W) Railroad M420 No. 2002, only four months old, is departing Valley Falls, Rhode Island, bound for the road's headquarters at Woonsocket in July 1974. The P&W dates to 1875 as one of the original roads leased by the New Haven. Penn Central took over New Haven in 1968, then went bankrupt in 1969. The stockholders took back their railroad, and have run it at a profit ever since.
Jim Boyd

In celebration of the 200th birthday of the United States, several railroads painted patriotic red-white-and-blue designs onto locomotives. Bangor & Aroostook (B&A) did this, and it was one of the few roads to name locomotives for actual patriots. The 1776 was named Jeremiah O'Brien, seen here at Perham, Maine, on September 30, 1976.
Mike Miterko

LEFT
On this day, December 8, 1988, motive power on the Central Vermont Railway (CV) was primarily GP9s. Two are idling at the Palmer engine terminal where the CV crosses Conrail at grade. In February 1995, the Central Vermont Railway was purchased by Railtex Corporation, which renamed it the New England Central.
Author photo

ABOVE
A pair of Maine Central GP38s lead the last run of St. Johnsbury freight train YR-1 past the ball signal guarding the Boston & Maine crossing at Whitefield, New Hampshire, on September 3, 1983. The ball signal is one of the earliest forms of train control systems, and this still-standing example is the last one in service.
Jim Shaughnessy

RIGHT
At 6,293 feet, Mount Washington is the highest peak in the eastern United States. On July 3, 1869, a cog railroad was opened to the top. The unique steam locomotives propel themselves with four cylinders driving a cog wheel that grips a rack laid between the rails. The railroad climbs 3,760 feet in only three miles. To keep the water close to level in the unique 0-2-2-0s that push the trains up the 37.41 per cent maximum grade, the boilers are at a ten-degree angle. Except for brief breaks during both world wars, the steam-only Mount Washington Cog Railway has operated continuously for 130 years. The Great Gulf was making this trip on July 9, 1996.
Author photo

THE SOUTHEAST

While the people and lifestyle in the southeastern United States may be leisurely and laid back, its railroading is as rough and rugged as anywhere in North America. Railroads such as the B&O and the South Carolina Railroad were pioneers, but iron rails soon spread and covered the region like kudzu. Railroading here also had a proud and independent spirit, but during the American Civil War it took a severe beating.

After the war, the network was reconstructed and well managed. Railroads in the south gained respect during the steam era, and they merged into powerful systems after dieselization. Indeed, as the twentieth century closes it is Norfolk Southern and CSX Transportation—successors to those post-civil war railroads—that have conquered the railroads of the North. The South is no slouch in topography, either. The steepest main line grade in America and the longest stretch of tangent track are in North Carolina. It has its own loop—Hiwassee in southeastern Tennessee—where a train must cross over itself to gain elevation. And lines like the Rathole south of Cincinnati and the old NC&St.L outside of Chattanooga would challenge the stoutest engine crews from the West.

LEFT
The most technically advanced steam locomotive in the southeast: a Norfolk & Western Class J 4-8-4. Designed and built by the N&W in its own Roanoke shops, it features a large combustion chamber and roller bearings on each critically balanced wheel and side rod. With 300psi boilers, the Js were the most powerful of all 4-8-4s.
Kenneth L. Miller Collection

THE SOUTHEAST

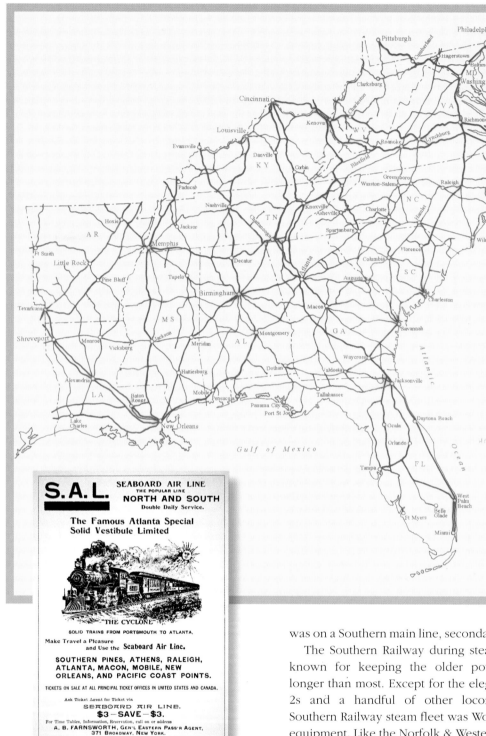

The railroads south of the Mason-Dixon line and the Ohio River, and east of the Mississippi, certainly had an adventurous history, more so than rail lines in any other region. Big-time railroading was born on the mid-Atlantic coast in the form of the Baltimore & Ohio and the South Carolina Railroad. Five-foot gauge was the most common in this region, and railroads spread like wildfire. The Civil War wreaked havoc and lines that were not battle-damaged were destroyed by the Northern armies. During the rebuilding, many smaller companies were merged and absorbed into other systems, creating a network of Class 1 railroads that survived into the 1960s.

In the mid-Atlantic region, railroads plowed inland; coal was the goal initially, then to extend west to the Ohio River and beyond. But the Appalachian Mountains were a formidable barrier. Four major railroads would build over and through the "Apple-chain" range. The Baltimore & Ohio and the Chesapeake & Ohio railroads were the first, and branches tapped the rich coal fields along the way. Both roads reach Chicago. Later, the Norfolk & Western built west from its namesake Atlantic coast town via Roanoke to tap the coal fields in West Virginia; it too built and accumulated enough trackage to reach Chicago.

Business boomed on these roads, so much so that financiers built other lines to compete. The Western Maryland headed west from Baltimore into the coal fields of northern West Virginia, and north to Connellsville, Pennsylvania (roughly near Pittsburgh). The Virginian built roughly parallel to the Norfolk & Western. Since these roads were constructed long after the Baltimore & Ohio and Norfolk & Western, respectively, they lacked right-of-way and had to build heavy main lines with many bridges, cuts and tunnels and moderate grades. These lines were indeed modern marvels.

In 1973 the Chesapeake & Ohio, having already gained control of the Baltimore & Ohio, merged to form the Chessie System. The merged road owned more than 90 per cent of the Western Maryland, and brought it into the fold and abandoned most of the duplicate trackage. Similarly, the Norfolk & Western bought the competing Virginian. Instead of abandonment, the Norfolk & Western took advantage of its superior grades and engineering. In places, the Norfolk & Western main line handles westbound empties, while the gently sloped Virginian is used to roll the coal to eastern ports.

Without a doubt, the dominant railroad in the South was the Southern Railway. Like the other roads, it was formed from dozens of smaller companies. Prudent management and frugal spending led to the Southern becoming a very well run and respected railroad. The Southern's tracks seemingly went everywhere; it stretched, in leisurely fashion, from Washington, D.C., to Richmond, Norfolk and Jacksonville in the east, to St. Louis, Memphis and New Orleans in the west. Just about any town worth its weight in freight was on a Southern main line, secondary or branch.

The Southern Railway during steam days was known for keeping the older power running longer than most. Except for the elegant PS4 4-6-2s and a handful of other locomotives, the Southern Railway steam fleet was World War I-era equipment. Like the Norfolk & Western, the diesel days on the Southern featured long hood forward operation. The Louisville & Nashville (L&N) was the railroad that best portrayed the South. It connected Cincinnati, St. Louis and Memphis with New Orleans, Mobile and Atlanta. The L & N, too, went most places, having been formed from literally dozens of smaller pre-civil war railroads. In the mix was the charming Nashville, Chattanooga & St. Louis, which called itself "the Dixie Line".

Along the coast two separate systems connected the State of Florida with the north, via Washington,

PRINCIPAL OPERATORS

Atlanta & St. Andrews Bay
Atlanta & West Point
Atlantic Coast Line (CSX)

Baltimore & Ohio (CSX)
Central of Georgia (NS)

Chesapeake & Ohio (CSX)
Chicago, Rock Island & Pacific
Florida East Coast
Georgia Railroad (CSX)
Gulf, Mobile & Ohio (IC)
Louisville & Nashville (CSX)
Missouri Pacific (UP)
Nashville, Chattanooga & St. Louis (CSX)

Norfolk & Western (NS)
Richmond, Fredericksburg & Potomac (CSX)
Seaboard Air Line (CSX)
Southern Railway (NS)
St. Louis San Francisco,
called the Cotton Belt (UP)
Western Maryland (CSX)

CONTEMPORARY OPERATORS

Amtrak
Burlington Northern Santa Fe
CSX Transportation
Illinois Central
Kansas City Southern
Norfolk Southern Corporation
Union Pacific

(MODERN MERGED IDENTITIES ARE IN PARENTHESES)

RIGHT
A small construction crew repairs damage to the Nashville, Chattanooga & St. Louis bridge over the Running Water Creek during the American Civil War. The NC&St.L main line was a vital link for the Confederate armies, since it connected with the Western & Atlantic at Chattanooga, and it extended northward to Nashville. Armies of both the North and the South quickly realized that the easiest way to cripple a railroad was to sabotage the bridges. The war taught America just how important the railroads were.
AAR photo, Salamander Picture Library

D.C. The Seaboard Air Line and the Atlantic Coast Line were nearly parallel, and the two companies competed for years (until they merged in 1967). Florida itself had its own railroad, the Florida East Coast. Begun in 1885 by Henry Flagler, he is largely responsible for developing Florida into the vacation hot-spot it remains today. His southward quest led him to build a spectacular arched bridge south of Miami that spanned the Everglades and the ocean to Key West. After many delays caused by hurricanes, the bridge was finished in 1912 but in 1935 it was damaged beyond practical repair by another hurricane. The Florida East Coast was later purchased by St. Joe Paper, which still owns it.

Merger mania swept through the region during the 1970s and 1980s. While this happened everywhere, it was in the southeast that the most old flags fell to create the biggest changes. It began with the Louisville & Nashville picking up the Nashville, Chattanooga & St. Louis in 1957. In 1967 the Seaboard Air Line merged with the Atlantic Coast Line to form Seaboard Coast Line. (This then merged in 1982 with the Louisville & Nashville to form the Seaboard System Railroad.)

Chessie System was formed in 1973, a holding company owning the Baltimore & Ohio, Chesapeake & Ohio and Western Maryland. In 1980, Chessie System merged with Seaboard Coast Line's parent company, Seaboard Coast Line

Industries, forming the Seaboard System Railroad. The Clinchfield, jointly formed by the Louisville & Nashville and Atlantic Coast Line, soon joined the family in 1983. In 1987 Seaboard System changed its name to CSX Transportation (C for Chessie, S for Seaboard and X for the multiplication of the two), which soon formally merged all of its remaining separate railroads into one name. CSX assumed 80 per cent of the Richmond, Fredericksburg & Potomac (it's ownership was shared by many southern railroads and the State of Virginia) with all of its mergers, and in 1995 it got the State of Virginia's shares. With the addition of the Richmond, Fredericksburg & Potomac, CSX Transportation became a 19,000-mile system with more than 3,000 locomotives.

In 1982, the Norfolk & Western and Southern Railway merged to become Norfolk Southern Corporation. That combination also included the old Norfolk Southern Railway in North Carolina, and other roads such as the Winston-Salem Southbound and many others. Including Norfolk Southern's holdings in the midwest, it operates a 14,700-mile system.

The big news in 1997 was that both Norfolk Southern and CSX would purchase and split northern rival Conrail, subject to the approval of the federal Surface Transportation Board. It appears that while the North won the civil war, the South won the railroads more than 130 years later.

The 4-4-0 wheel arrangement was popular in the South before the civil war. Here we see a shiny No.29 of the Louisville & Nashville pausing in the 1860s in what appears to be downtown Nashville. During this era locomotives were assigned to engineers, and each man treated it as if it were his own. The antlers over the headlight suggest that this hogger is a hunter on his off day.
Peter Newark's American Pictures

The Baltimore & Ohio, of course, had a large presence in its namesake city's harbor area. This scene from the 1880s shows B&O's large complex at Locust Point in South Baltimore, not far from the Mount Clare shops. Immigrants, who had arrived at piers eight or nine and had been processed in the immigrant center within the brick building to the left, are preparing to board trains for the American West. Immigrants founded America, and the constant influx of people and creativity from around the world helped create the inventions that built the railroad industry.
B&O Railroad photo, MARS

ABOVE

A pair of Southern
Railway 2-8-0s are
waiting at Alexandria,
Virginia, in 1895, and
ready to roll with another
freight train. By the end of
the nineteenth century,
the Southern was a big
believer in the 2-8-0, and
it ultimately owned
hundreds of them.
*Charles E. Fisher photo,
T.W. Dixon, Jr. Collection*

LEFT

The station at Alderson,
West Virginia, was built in
1896. This reflects the
standard station design
on the Chesapeake &
Ohio Railway as
introduced in the 1890s.
*T.W. Dixon, Jr.,
photo, C&O Historical
Society Collection*

LEFT
The "Gandy Dancer" earned his place in American folklore. Work was scarce in the South after the Civil War, and many black men looking for employment found themselves lining and maintaining track all over the United States. In this 1880s view along the Seaboard Air Line Railroad in the Carolinas, we see a typical track crew apparently out changing rail. The days were long and the work was hard.
C&O Historical Society Collection

RIGHT
Bananas were always big business for the railroads. Arriving by boats at southern ports from South and Central America, bananas were shipped north in refrigerated boxcars. This scene from Baltimore in 1910 shows bunches of bananas being unloaded from Pennsylvania Railroad reefers. The two gentlemen in jackets—inspectors for the US Food & Drug Administration—are inspecting in the presence of a local police officer. Shifting bananas could be dangerous work, as poisonous spiders would occasionally travel within the bunches.
National Archives, Salamander Picture Library

BELOW
The Atlantic Coast Line owned many 4-4-0s in the nineteenth century. This one was built by Baldwin in 1888 for the Western Branch Railway as the No.2; it was later sold to the Norfolk & Carolina Railroad, which renumbered it to 401. In 1900 it was transferred to the ACL, which renumbered it to 442. The ACL sold it in 1910. Judging from the pile of wood, the engine is just starting its run.
C.L. Goolsby Collection

ABOVE
The Rogers Locomotive Works of Paterson, New Jersey, built this classic 4-4-0 in 1882 for the Savannah, Florida & Western Railway. It was captured on film during a station stop at Crescent City, Florida, in 1899. The locomotive was sold to the Atlantic Coast Line in 1902; renumbered to 472, it was scrapped in 1906. Rogers was well known among railroads for its fine workmanship and reliable locomotives.
ACL photo, C.L. Goolsby Collection

LEFT
A westbound train making a station stop at the Baltimore & Ohio station in Cumberland, Maryland, one of America's oldest industrial centers. Indeed, the first iron rails in America were rolled near here at Mount Savage. The station was built on the banks of the Potomac, and the B&O shared it with the Western Maryland Railroad. *Peter Newark's American Pictures*

ABOVE

The Baldwin Locomotive Works was perhaps better known for its 2-8-0s than almost any other wheel arrangement. Baldwin mastered mass production techniques, and it built many thousands of 2-8-0s of various sizes for US and foreign railroads. When the US Army urgently needed 2-8-0s for World War I, Baldwin designed and delivered the first one in twenty days, and it built more than 300 of them in a single month. Just under 2,000 had been constructed by the war's end. In 1913 this example was on the Southern Railway at Alexandria, Virginia.
T.W. Dixon, Jr., Collection

RIGHT

A string of brand-new 2-8-2s built by Baldwin for the Baltimore & Ohio are being looked over in 1915. Built to the specifications of the United States Railway Administration, these light Mikados turned out to be one of the more practical and successful designs for the job they were intended to do. Light 2-8-2s of this design, and some that are very similar, could be found on many large railroads all over the USA.
Baldwin photo, Salamander Picture Library

RIGHT, INSET

An Atlantic Coast Line freight train is pausing at Rooks, North Carolina, during June 1914. The 4-4-0 leading this train was built by Rogers during September 1885. The cars with screen doors are ventilated boxcars, especially designed for the transport of produce, mainly watermelons. Open air freight platforms were quite common in the South. *ACL photo, C.L. Goolsby Collection*

ABOVE

Long strings of coal trains emerged from the mountains and on to market via railroad, at the rate of fifty-five tons per hopper car when this view was made. Coal was the heart and soul of many railroads in the mid-Atlantic states: homes and offices were heated with it, electricity was generated by burning it, and the locomotives used it all over the country. But it was the railroads in the South that got paid the most for hauling the coal. *C&O Historical Society Collection*

LEFT

No pre-war scene from the South is more typical than this: a 4-6-2 whisking a passenger train at track speed. In tow are a railway post office car, a mail storage car, and eight passenger cars. The 4-6-2 wheel arrangement was known as the Pacific-type; railroads in the East and South used them in passenger service even after the development of the 4-8-2 and 4-8-4.
William Kratville

ABOVE

The biggest locomotives on the Southern Railway were articulated 2-8-8-2s from Baldwin. Here, one of them approaches Atlanta, Georgia, with a freight train. Because the lead engine swivels under the boiler, most Mallets have a very smooth ride and are easy on the track structure. Many smaller, rigid-frame locomotives are rough on track and engine crews.
T.W. Dixon, Jr., Collection

LEFT

The dining car was an important tradition of train travel. Indeed, some roads were better known for their chefs than for their equipment or scenery. This photo aboard the Baltimore & Ohio's dining car Mount Vernon in January 1924 could have been made on any major railroad in America. The hardwood chairs, monogrammed napkins and custom menus were not unusual. Today, a growing industry is recreating these days when dining on rails was an experience.
B&O Railroad photo, MARS

ABOVE

A 1930s scene showing a Florida East Coast train heading south over the Long Key Bridge that stretched from the Florida Everglades to Key West. The bridge was completed in 1912 after great difficulty; contemporary accounts of it claim "that it seemed to run off the end of the Earth." FEC's founder Henry Flagler built a railroad in the Sunshine State, and in doing so he helped to develop Florida. This bridge was damaged beyond practical repair by a hurricane in 1935. *FEC photo, Salamander Picture Library*

RIGHT

Atlantic Coast Line 4-6-2 1536 is getting under way at Augusta, Georgia, with a ten-car passenger train on November 29, 1933. This is the Wednesday service on the Palmetto Limited, Train No.28, which operated between Savannah and Washington, D.C. The ACL had 1,000 miles of main line between Richmond and Miami; it got access to the nation's capital via the Richmond, Fredericksburg & Potomac, while access to Miami was over the Florida East Coast. *Kevin T. Farrell photo, C.L.Goolsby Collection*

LEFT
Built by EMC in 1935 as a boxcab diesel for the B&O, the No. 50 is a direct predecessor of the E-series streamliners. B&O later transferred it to the Chicago & Alton to run as the Abraham Lincoln.
B&O photo, Salamander Picture Library

TOP
The Southern Railway had a reputation for excellent track, as can be seen in this 1935 view at Seminary, Virginia, as a light Pacific gets a three car train underway, the first car being a Railway Post Office car.
T.W. Dixon, Jr., Collection

ABOVE
On the Southern Railway, the steam queens were the PS-4 class 4-6-2s in passenger service. This view from the summer of 1936 shows No. 1399 at the Ivy City engine terminal, north of Washington, D.C.
Southern Railway, MARS

The flagship train on the Chesapeake & Ohio was the George Washington. Here the train pauses at White Sulphur Springs, West Virginia, on its nightly run between Washington, D.C., and Cincinnati during 1935. The drumhead had no lettering, just the portrait of Washington. The C&O used a colonial motif because George Washington, the man, was actually president of one of the predecessor companies of the railroad and the C&O canal. The C&O was loyal to George the train, it having been the last C&O passenger train to operate, suspended on Amtrak's first day in 1971.
C&O Railway photo, C&O Historical Society Collection.

Chesapeake & Ohio's first full-service name train was introduced on May 11, 1889, as the Fast Flying Virginian. Its splendid narrow-vestibule cars were painted bright orange and maroon. The FFV put the C&O on the list of classy passenger haulers and she stood the test of time, surviving both world wars and into the diesel era, finally dying on May 12, 1968. In this 1936 scene, the FFV is coasting to a stop in the fog at Montgomery, West Virginia.
C&O Historical Society Collection

One of the Southern Railway's elegant PS-4 Pacific types rolls a passenger train across the Potomac River Bridge on its northbound run into Washington, D.C., in April 1937. Five major roads offered direct services into the capital at that time: the Southern, the Richmond, Fredericksburg & Potomac, the Pennsylvania, the C&O and B&O. The Seaboard Air Line and Atlantic Coast Line handed their trains to the RF&P near Richmond. *T.W. Dixon, Jr., Collection*

The Seaboard Air Line picked one of the most striking paint designs for its Orange Blossom Special and other long-distance trains. This E6 was built by Electro-Motive in 1938, a graceful design created by Leland Knickerbocker and Paul Meyer of EMD's styling section. When a railroad ordered its first diesels, it was presented with several options for an appealing paint design. Seaboard's "citrus" livery was arguably among the best. *EMD photo, MARS*

BELOW

In this stunning publicity pose from 1941, we see the first of Norfolk & Western's Class J 4-8-4s, No.600, with its shiny new passenger train in front of the Blue Ridge Mountains of Virginia. The Class Js were just about the ultimate development of the 4-8-4: one pulled a 1025-ton test train at 110mph in Virginia—that's a feat usually reserved for eighty-inch drivered locomotives.
N&W photo, MARS

RIGHT

The Chesapeake & Ohio used many Mallets (pronounced Malley) to move its coal and freight trains over the mountains. Here, in the summer of 1948, we see an H-7 class 2-8-8-2 cresting the grade at Alleghany, Virginia, with a manifest in tow. Thick black plumes indicated inefficient combustion, so most managers demanded that the engineers run with a clean smoke stack whenever possible.
Gordon Roth

RIGHT
The Southern Railway, too, got caught up in the era of streamlined steam, and it hired designer Otto Kuhler to put a skyline casing on one of its PS-4 4-6-2s in 1941. This photo shows one of them at the Ivy City engine terminal during 1948. Kuhler had also been enlisted to design the Lehigh Valley's Asa Packer and the Milwaukee's Hiawatha locomotives. Southern's streamlined PS-4s were unusual in that they remained streamlined beyond World War II.
T.W. Dixon, Jr., Collection

ABOVE

At Ivy City terminal in the 1950s, locomotives from each of the roads serving Washington, D.C., could be found laying over between trips, and such line-ups have become legendary. Witness this view of four streamlined locomotives from three different railroads. On the ready track this night are (left to right) a Southern Railway E7, a Baltimore & Ohio E7, a Chesapeake & Ohio E8 and a Southern Railway E8, all built by Electro-Motive Division of General Motors.
Jim Shaughnessy

RIGHT

Baltimore & Ohio's bridge spanning the Susquehanna River at Havre de Grace, Maryland, is a massive and graceful structure that gained the B&O access to Wilmington, Delaware, from Baltimore. In 1955, the railroad posed this publicity photo with the regular train on the Havre de Grace bridge featuring a clean set of A-B-B F7s and the B&O boxcars at the head end. The Susquehanna River was also crossed by the rival Pennsylvania Railroad near this spot on a similar bridge. Both bridges remained in use at the end of the 1990s.
B&O Railroad photo, MARS

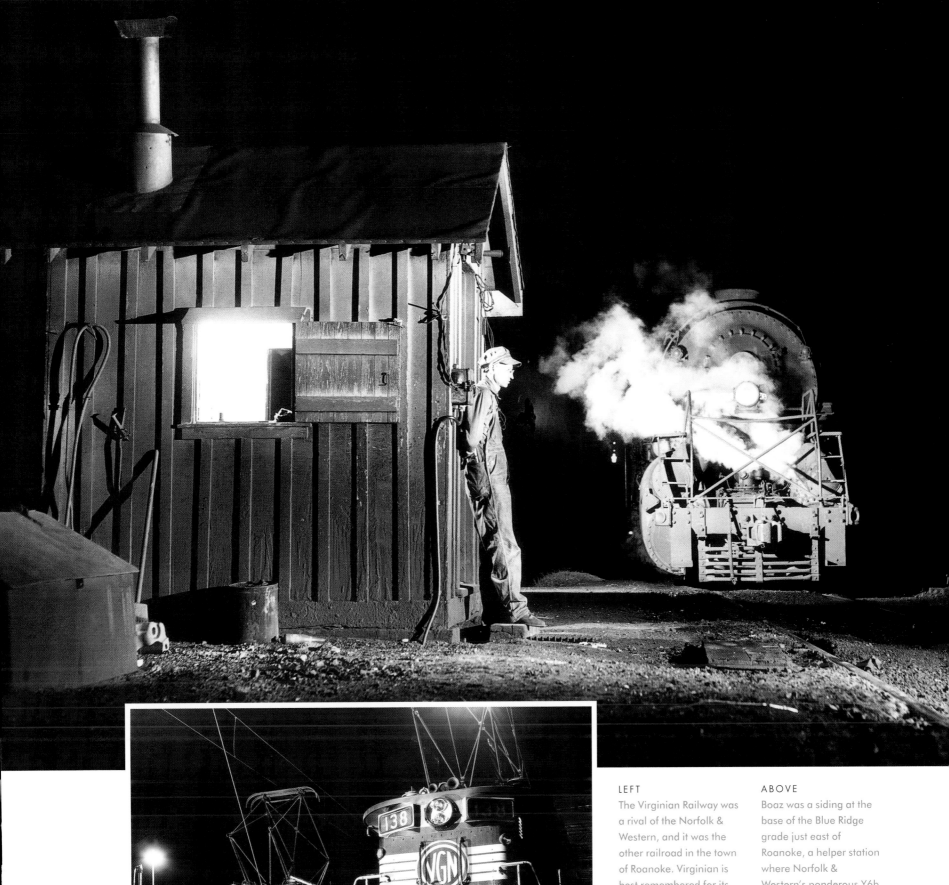

LEFT
The Virginian Railway was a rival of the Norfolk & Western, and it was the other railroad in the town of Roanoke. Virginian is best remembered for its 134-mile electrified main line from Roanoke west to Mullens. Virginian's last electrics were 3300hp E33s from General Electric, two of which are shown at the Roanoke terminal during August 1958.
Kenneth L. Miller Collection

ABOVE
Boaz was a siding at the base of the Blue Ridge grade just east of Roanoke, a helper station where Norfolk & Western's ponderous Y6b 2-8-8-2s were staged and watered while waiting for eastbound coal trains that needed a boost to get over the top. On a hot August night in 1958, a Y6b 2169 and its hostler are simmering.
Jim Shaughnessy

ABOVE

A spectacular stretch of railroad is the Baltimore & Ohio's Cumberland to Cincinnati main line, known as B&O's West End. Part of the line climbs one side of the valley containing the Cheat River near Rowlesburg, West Virginia. In November 1967, three EMD locomotives have a westbound coal train on the roll at Rowlesburg, just out of M&K Junction where the track to Morgantown splits from the main line. The grade here reaches 2 per cent.
Jim Boyd

RIGHT

Style mattered in the years after World War II, and many railroads had their own brands, not least the Seaboard Air Line. It experimented with numerous paint designs, and it kept the images of its passenger, freight and terminal locomotives colorful, and separate. Witness this November 1967 line-up in Richmond, Virginia, of (left to right) the passenger E7, the freight GP7, and the Baldwin RS12 road and yard switcher.
Jim Boyd

LEFT
The eighty-one-mile Atlanta & St. Andrews Bay Railroad (A&St.AB), which opened in 1908, was one of the first railroads in North America to dieselize, with a pair of Alco road switchers in 1941. In the 1990s, the all-EMD fleet amounted to twelve units. This five-unit EMD-built consist at the Panama City, Florida, shops in April 1973 shows three of the 1950s-era units in the foreground and two of the newer locomotives in the distance.
Mike Miterko

ABOVE
The Clinchfield Railroad knitted its way through the Appalachian Mountains by tunneling and filling and bridging and twisting. It connected the coal fields of eastern Kentucky with Spartanburg, South Carolina. But the Carolina, Clinchfield & Ohio, known simply as the Clinchfield, made up in engineering and performance for what it lacked in distance. At its peak 100,000 tons of coal rolled daily through some tough country.
Jim Boyd

RIGHT

Norfolk Southern built a rail dynasty in the South, and by the 1990s it was one of the biggest money-makers in North America; it is one of the few considered by Wall Street to be revenue adequate—profitable enough to recover its cost of capital. That's a complicated term, but the fact is that Norfolk Southern is an efficient operation and an industry leader. Among its hallmarks, as seen in this April 25, 1987, view from the Blue Ridge Parkway east of Roanoke, are well-manicured tracks and locomotives equipped to run in either direction, which saves having to turn them at the end of a trip.
Author photo

RIGHT

Norfolk Southern intermodal Train 127 is southbound in Ruffin, North Carolina, the day after a January 1987 snowstorm. Ruffin is located on the former Southern Railway's Washington, D.C. to Atlanta main line. Before the Norfolk Southern merger, this was the Southern Railway's major artery to the northern railroads, and it is no less important today.
Doug Koontz

RIGHT

Richmond, Virginia, is one of the few places where three railroads cross. The phenomenon was created in 1901 when the Chesapeake & Ohio completed its bridge over the Richmond waterfront, which happened to cross the Seaboard Air Line's bridge over the Southern Railway's West Point line. The first locomotive pose happened in 1906 and the last one (here), before the big mergers, on July 19, 1983.
Jim Boyd

THE MIDWEST

More than any other city, Chicago is America's railroad junction. Almost every railroad got to Chicago somehow to interchange traffic, and the volume was so great that two railroads were built to handle little more than pure interchange traffic between the major railroads. At its peak after World War II, the switching district occupied an area roughly the size of Rhode Island. It used 8,000 miles of track and interchanged roughly 600 freight trains daily.

It has also been written that no city had more railroad stations than Chicago. The city benefited from rail travel in that long-distance passenger trains all stopped there. Riders had to transfer between stations, and they spent money or spent the night in the process. Chicago and the midwest was also the capital of the interurban, mostly passenger-hauling, systems that connected a string of small cities and towns. These lines had the track speed of the steam roads, with equipment resembling the trolley cars.

The railroads between Chicago and St. Louis, and to the west and north, served primarily the farmers of the Great Plains states. Many railroads built through the grange, and in the early part of the twentieth century these roads became known as "grangers."

LEFT
Chicago & North Western's (C&NW) Twin Cities 400 curves out of North Western Station in Chicago behind a pair of EMC E3s in 1939. The 400s were named in reference to the train's steam-era schedule from Chicago to the Twin Cities: 400 miles in 400 minutes. The C&NW trains competed with the Milwaukee's Hiawathas and the Burlington's Zephyrs. Lake Street tower can be seen to the right of the distant signal bridge, while the squarish building at the extreme left is the Merchandise Mart, once the largest commercial structure in America.
Chicago & North Western Railway, MARS

THE MIDWEST

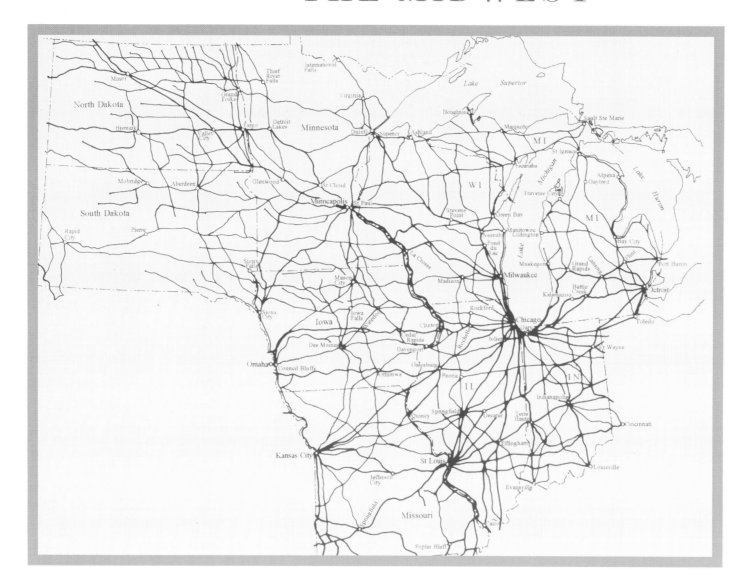

The heartbeat of the midwest is Chicago, and Chicago is a railroad town—the original gateway to the West. After the American Civil War, three major railroads connected New York and Chicago (the New York Central, Pennsylvania, and the Erie). Many small railroads interchanged with similar-sized roads in the east to carry freight into Chicago. Eastern "regional" railroads like the Lackawanna and the Lehigh Valley used connections with midwestern roads like the Nickel Plate, Pere Marquette, and Wabash to reach Chicago. These smaller roads honed scheduling to become formidable competitors. Once in Chicago, the freight was interchanged and by the turn of the century five railroads reached the Pacific coast, and a host of others could carry freight anywhere west. Chicago interchanged more individual railroads than any other North American city. Let's look at some of them.

The main line of mid-America was the Illinois Central. It stretched from Chicago to New Orleans, and operated lines to St. Louis and Birmingham, Alabama, where the Central of Georgia brought Illinois Central trains to Jacksonville, Florida. After the civil war it was a key player in the largest migration in American history, as freed slaves went north in search of a better life. The Illinois Central had also built a main line from Chicago west across Iowa to Omaha; the road embodied much of the personality of midwest railroading: images of orange-and-chocolate streamlined diesels pulling the Panama Limited or the City of New Orleans will live long in the minds of anyone who grew up in the land of Lincoln.

Roughly parallel to the Illinois Central was the Gulf, Mobile & Ohio, which cut diagonally across Illinois to reach St. Louis, and it continued south to Mobile, Alabama, with main line spurs to New Orleans, Birmingham and Montgomery. It was the sum of many famous predecessors, including the Gulf, Mobile & Northern, the Mobile & Ohio and the Chicago & Alton. The Illinois Central would engulf the Gulf, Mobile & Ohio in the 1970s to form Illinois Central Gulf.

Colorful railroads covered the Great Plains west and northwest of Chicago. Most prominent was the Chicago & North Western, with roots dating to 1840. Its main lines reached west to Omaha, north to Green Bay and Duluth, and northwest through Minneapolis into the Black Hills of the Dakotas and Wyoming. Also, Chicago & North Western had a web of branches throughout the prairies. Its distinctive steam roster and colorful diesels were a dominant image.

The Chicago, Milwaukee, St. Paul & Pacific, better known as the Milwaukee Road, was nearly as web-like across the grange, but it eventually built all the way to the Pacific coast through the northern frontier states. The Milwaukee Road was a granger at heart, connecting the Dakotas and Minnesota, Wisconsin and Iowa with Chicago. It became well known for its streamlined steam locomotives, but perhaps the Milwaukee items

that made the greatest impression to train watchers were the lineside "Reduce to 90 m.p.h." signs.

A neighbor of the Milwaukee Road was the Minneapolis, St. Paul & Saulte Ste. Marie, formed in the 1870s by Twin Cities' millers trying to avoid Chicago and the high freight rates charged by other railroads. This company was nicknamed the "Saulte" Line, pronounced "Soo Line," and the "Soo" would purchase nearby smaller roads, such as the Wisconsin Central and the Duluth, South Shore & Atlantic. In 1961 this trio was formally incorporated as the Soo Line.

As time went on, more railroads formed, further adding to the spaghetti bowl of trackage in the upper midwest. The Chicago Great Western called itself the Corn Belt Route. It was a Y-shaped system that connected Chicago and Minneapolis with Omaha and Kansas City, coming together at a huge triangle of track in northern Iowa. The Chicago Great Western was an innovator, having tried gas-electric rail cars as early as 1910 and building one of the very first streamliners. It dieselized early with a variety of motive power and color schemes. The Chicago Great Western was big time railroading in the prairies.

Another colorful regional was the Minneapolis & St. Louis, which avoided Chicago but brought Twin Cities traffic through the "Peoria Gateway" south of Chicago. It had its own nest of Iowa branch lines; as did the Chicago, Rock Island & Pacific which also went north to Minneapolis, but went as far west as Tucumcari, New Mexico, to connect with the Southern Pacific and south to the Texas gulf coast, with 8,000 miles of track in all.

The Chicago, Burlington & Quincy bragged about going everywhere west, but in Illinois and Iowa it was a true super railroad. It built a four-track raceway westward out of Chicago that split into three main lines to reach the Mississippi River cities of St. Louis, Quincy and Burlington. It went everywhere west from there. The "Q's" steam was legendary, and it helped EMC develop the streamliners. It was the main freight line between the Twin Cities and Chicago, and it brought the lion's share of Great Northern and Northern Pacific traffic to the Windy City.

The Atchison, Topeka & Santa Fe was begun by Cyrus K. Holliday to connect its namesake cities and it grew to become the quickest trip for freight and passengers between Chicago and Los Angeles. Its steam locomotives were among the best in the land, and passengers regarded its Super Chief as one of America's grandest streamliners.

Great changes came to the midwest. In the 1970s, the Northern Pacific, Great Northern, Chicago, Burlington & Quincy (and the Spokane, Portland & Seattle and Frisco) formed the Burlington Northern (BN). In 1997, BN bought the Santa Fe. The Rock Island drifted into bankruptcy, but much of it survives as short lines. The Chicago & North Western absorbed the Chicago Great Western and Minneapolis & St. Louis, which Union Pacific engulfed in 1995. The Wabash and Nickel Plate were folded into the Norfolk & Western which merged with the Southern to form Norfolk Southern Corporation. Michigan's Pere Marquette joined Chesapeake & Ohio, which merged with Baltimore & Ohio and others to form Chessie System, which later became CSX Transportation. The Soo Line bought the Milwaukee Road, then abandoned its original line and sold much of it to Wisconsin Central Limited. Confused? Today's Soo runs the old Milwaukee Road, and the original Soo became a highly profitable regional railroad.

LEFT

The Pioneer was the first locomotive purchased by the Chicago & North Western's predecessor, Galena & Chicago Union Railroad, in 1848. Its history is obscure; it was built by Baldwin for the Towanda (N.Y) Railroad as the No.4, Batavia, around 1843. Possibly the first built with a steel frame, it is the oldest surviving Baldwin locomotive and is in the care of the Chicago Historical Society.
MARS

BELOW

The Northern Pacific was a fledgling railroad in 1880 when this photo was taken. Large rivers were not then bridgeable so railcars had to be barged across on ferries. This is the Missouri River at Bismarck, North Dakota, and the little Baldwin 0-4-0 has just shoved a string of boxcars onto the ferry. The empty flat cars are "reachers," used to keep the weight of the locomotive off of the float bridge.
MARS

ABOVE
On the last day of 1886, the City of Fort Madison, Iowa, granted the Chicago, Santa Fe & California Railroad the right to construct a railroad in that town. Work began next day, and this scene along the Mississippi River at Fort Madison shows one of the typical methods of constructing fill: building a wood-pyle trestle and filling dirt around it. The railroad fill also acted as a levee in the event of a rise in Big Muddy.
MARS

RIGHT
Railroads endeavored to make its parlor, club and chair cars appear like the lobbies and lounges of the world's finest hotels. This is the lounge section of the Centennial Club Car in 1890s' motif. This car was in service on Santa Fe's Kansas City Chief, a luxury Kansas City to Chicago daily train. Note the gas lights along the walls and hanging from the ceiling, used in the days before Edison's electric lights became practical on the railways.
Santa Fe Railway, MARS

RIGHT
The Black Hills district of western South Dakota was laced with early railroads in pursuit of the revenues from hauling precious metals. This scene from the 1880s, near the mines of Deadwood, shows the Chicago, Burlington & Quincy passenger depot, crossed by the main line of the Fremont, Elkorn & Missouri Valley Railroad, which was crossed by a mining railroad. The FE&MV was purchased by the Chicago & North Western in 1902, while the CB&Q is the biggest part of today's Burlington Northern Santa Fe.
MARS

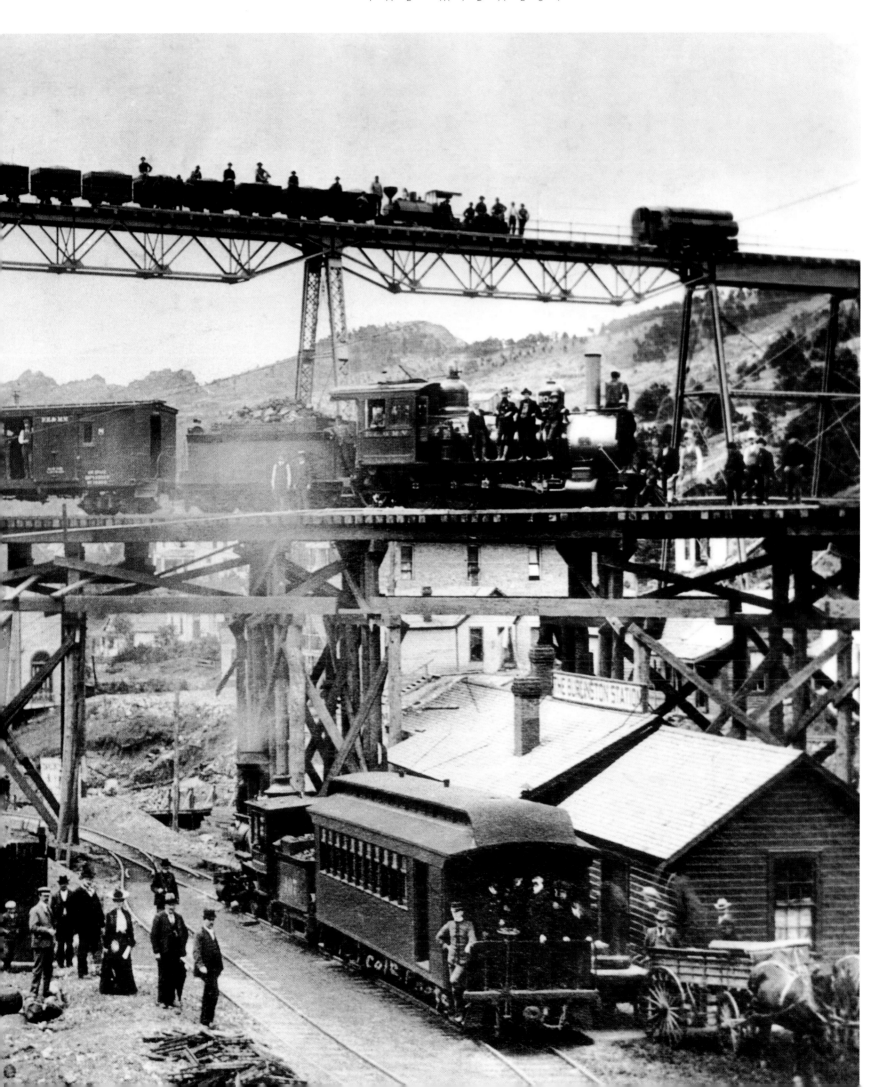

ABOVE

It is May 21, 1895, at 5:35 p.m., and we are witnessing the beginning of a Chicago rush hour on the Illinois Central Railroad. The IC's commuter trains operated from Chicago southward toward Kankakee. Steam was the rule until IC installed electric catenary and in 1926 began operating electric multiple unit cars. Painted Pullman-green and run in multi-car consist, this was one of the first electric commuter systems, and it set many standards that others would follow.
IC photo, MARS

LEFT

Cotton has been a financial staple of the economy for as long as there's been an America, and the railroads hauled tons of it north to textile mills. This scene from the late-1870s gives an accurate impression of the volumes of cotton that shipped during harvest season.

It is quite likely that everyone in this photo is either a railroad employee or a cotton hand, as it predates the knuckle couplers and air brakes of the 1880s. This is the Missouri Pacific yard in St. Louis, Missouri.
MP photo, MARS

RIGHT

A Northern Pacific passenger train is heading north over the steel bridge crossing Bohemian Flats near the University of Minnesota in Minneapolis, circa 1900. The track on this bridge was relocated, and the bridge abandoned, during a massive university expansion in the 1920s. Wooden consists such as this would soon be phased out with the development of steel underframes and carbodies during the first decade of the 1900s. This region of the country is known for its beer, and breweries were numerous; behind the bridge in this scene is the Minneapolis Brewing Company.

Minneapolis Journal photo, Minnesota Historical Society collection

RIGHT

The empire builder himself, James J. Hill (center), posed for this photo with his engineer and fireman from the William Crooks. The two gentleman at the right are Edwin Nelson and John P. Nelson. The St. Paul & Pacific was the first railroad in the upper midwest. Hill purchased it to form the basis of his Great Northern Railway. Hill extended this line to reach the Pacific and also built the Northern Pacific Railroad.

Minneapolis Journal photo, Minnesota Historical Society collection

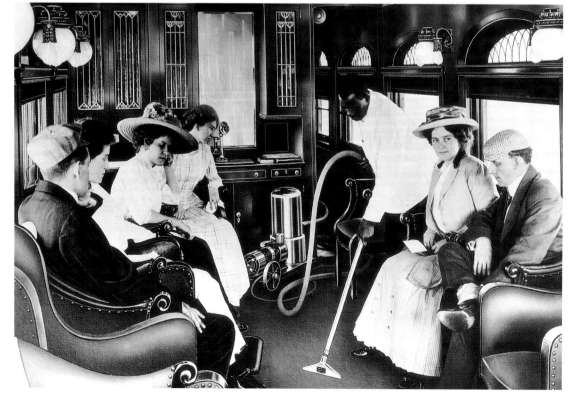

The parlor section of many observation-lounge cars at the turn of the century exuded elegance only seen by the public in the best hotels or on the finest cruise ships. Of course, riders paid extra fare to ride in such a conveyance. In addition to the inlaid wood and leaded glass found on traditional parlor cars, this one has many modern innovations of the time: electric lights and fans, a telephone, and a vacuum cleaner, too! Behind that wall would be a dining room, then two or three sleeping compartments.
MARS

ABOVE
Three Chicago, Burlington & Quincy switch engines and their crews pose in front of the former station at Pacific Junction in Iowa in 1905. "P Junk" is where the Kansas City-to-Council Bluffs main line crosses the line to Lincoln, Nebraska, and where trains bound for Omaha can turn north to follow the Missouri River. The locomotive on the left is an E-class 0-4-0, and the two on the right are both G-class 0-6-0s.
Northern Pacific photos, MARS

The rear platform was a highlight of the typical observation-lounge car. Usually ten riders would fill a car such as this one, owned by the Soo Line. The lounge is located just inside the door to the observation platform; the sleeping compartments are located at the other end of this car, and in the car ahead of it. The dining room windows at the center of the car are raised to keep people on station platforms from casually looking in at the diners.
Minnesota Historical Society collection, Salamander Picture Library

Times were tough before World War I, causing many men to take to the road in search of work, or to just get away. Such men were called hobos, a name derived from the term Hoe Boys and the work that was usually available on track-side farms. This many hobos on one train is unusual, but their wanderlust is not. At Hecla, South Dakota, this train is heading to Oakes, North Dakota, on Thursday, August 13, 1914. Most of these men would get off before riding that far.
Hersey & Hersey photo, Salamander Picture Library

BELOW

The Sunshine Special, Train 32, was Missouri Pacific's prestigious train from Shreveport, Louisiana, to St. Louis. This publicity photo was posed using Alco-built 4-6-2 No.6423 pulling a heavyweight consist with Pullman sleepers and a diner. This 1920s scene is near Middlebrook, Missouri, deep within the Arcadia Valley. With the valve gear in full forward, the engineer is about to widen out on the throttle to get this train through the gradient S-curves to reach Bismark, Missouri. *MP photo, MARS*

LEFT

Chicago Union Station was one of the midwest's biggest and busiest, serving the Pennsylvania, the Burlington and the Chicago & Alton from the south, and the Milwaukee Road from the north—yet it was only one of eight major stations in the Windy City. It is unusual in that it is made up of two separate structures, looking almost unrelated, that are bisected by Canal Street. In the foreground is the concourse, and behind it is the main waiting room with railroad offices above it. The tracks are below street level. *AAR photo, Salamander Picture Library.*

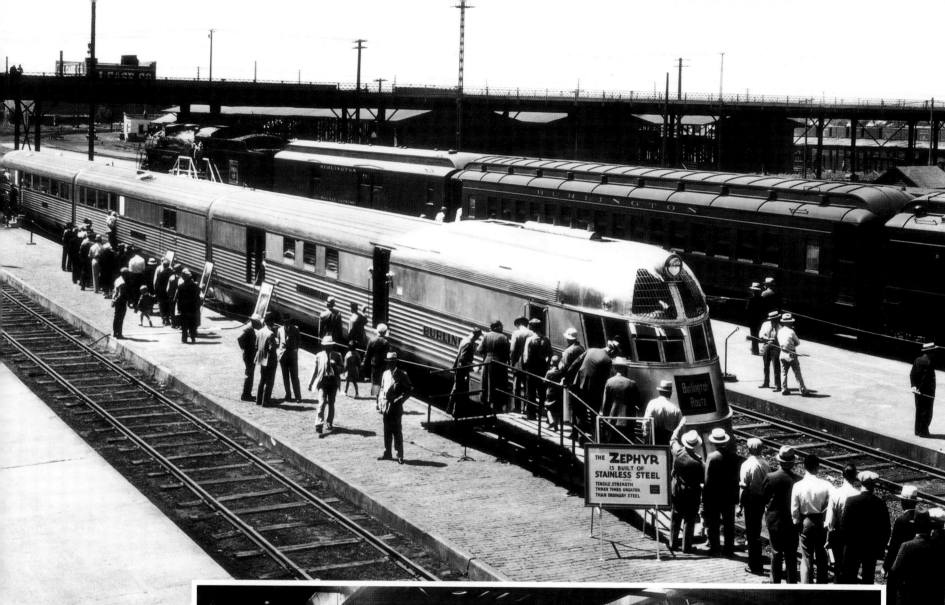

The Chicago, Burlington & Quincy wowed the crowds when it debuted its shiny, aircraft-like trainset, poetically named Zephyr. In 1934 the prototype toured the country and is seen here at Lincoln, Nebraska. This diesel-powered novelty had its critics until it made a dawn-to-dusk, non-stop run from Denver to Chicago to break through a ribbon opening the 1934 World's Fair. It averaged 77.4 miles per hour and beat the steam schedule by twelve hours. *CB&Q photo, TRH Pictures collection*

ABOVE
Chicago, Burlington & Quincy's Twin Zephyrs 9901 and 9902 posed side by side in Chicago Union Station in 1935, just after being built and only a year after the famous Pioneer Zephyr 9900. The shiny little trains zipped between Chicago and the Twin Cities to compete with the fast 400s of the Chicago & North Western and the Hiawatha trains of the Milwaukee Road. The success of these trainsets led EMC to develop the diesels that would revolutionize railroading in less than twenty years. *Association of American Railroads, MARS*

LEFT
The Milwaukee Road was proud of its streamlined A-class 4-4-2s for the Hiawatha passenger trains. With eighty-four-inch driving wheels, this oil-burning locomotive was a speedster capable of long stretches of 100mph running, and became the first to run in three-figure speeds routinely. Identified only by the 1 on the nose, the christening in 1935 was marked by the Milwaukee Road shop employees forming a human "M." *Milwaukee Road photo, University of Washington Libraries collection*

RIGHT
Another distinctive art deco element of the Hiawatha were the slope-backed lounge cars that punctuated the trainsets. Referred to as "beaver tail" observation cars, they featured a spacious and luxurious lounge, as seen in this 1935 view.

The sleek orange train with maroon and gray striping looked classy over the prairies as it flew past at more than 100mph. The Milwaukee Road's way side signs—"Reduce to 90"—are legendary. *Milwaukee Road photo, University of Washington Libraries collection*

LEFT
As the Milwaukee Road's high speed Chicago-Milwaukee Hiawathas got longer, the railroad needed to replace the powerful 4-4-2s with the F-7 class 4-6-4, built by Alco in 1938 and styled by Otto Kuhler. The 104 was nearly new in this September 24, 1938, view. The F-7 was capable of 120mph, and wheeled eighteen-car consists at 100mph with ease. *Milwaukee Public Library, MARS*

ABOVE
Industrial designer Otto Kuhler not only designed the locomotives for the Hiawatha, but also the car interiors and exteriors. This is the lounge car, dubbed the "Tip Top Tap" car. The common style of the streamliner era was based on the art deco architecture of the period, itself inspired by the discovery of King Tuts tomb in 1922. *Milwaukee Road photo, University of Washington Libraries collection*

LEFT
A 1937 scene of the yards in Milwaukee, Wisconsin. The locomotives in the immediate foreground are in service. The single locomotive on the second track is a brand new S-3 class 4-8-4 No.239, just arrived from Baldwin in Philadelphia. Those lined up with the smoke stacks capped on the far side of the new locomotive are in storage or retirement.
Electro-Motive photo, author collection

RIGHT
A streamlined Chicago & North Western A-4 class 4-6-4 No.4003 is leading the Omahan out of North Western Station in Chicago during March 1947. The C&NW's 4-6-4s were similar to the Milwaukee Road 4-6-4s. Both could roll a long passenger train as fast as track speed permitted.
Union Pacific Museum

RIGHT
World War II was nearly over when this photo of Missouri Pacific's Sunshine Special was made, showing it in the dawn's early light rolling through the St. Louis suburbs en route to the Gateway City, having originated in Texarkana the previous evening. The train had grown since the 1920s (see page 118), expanding to fourteen cars and rating Missouri Pacific's handsome and capable 5340.
Union Pacific Museum

RIGHT
Union Pacific endorsed
articulateds with
enthusiasm. Together
with the American
Locomotive Company, UP
developed a 4-6-6-4
design that was as close
to perfection, relative to
the job asked of it, as any
in the land. Built in 1942,
the 3964 is representative
of the Challenger-type.
These locomotives were
used on passenger and
freight trains system-wide
Union Pacific photo, MARS

BELOW

In addition to the 4-6-6-4s, another well-liked locomotive on Union Pacific was the FEF-3 Class 4-8-4s. These eighty-drivered Northern-types had a 300 p.s.i boiler pressure, and they could maintain 100mph with a sixteen-car train. Here we see the 836 blasting westward out of Omaha Union Station with the twelve-car consist of Train 23 during January 1953. The 4-8-4s were UP's last steam locomotive purchases, and the last of this batch, 844 built in 1944, holds the distinction of having never been retired.
William Kratville

LEFT

The Chicago, Burlington & Quincy had a diverse roster of steam locomotives, some more appealing than others. Here Burlington 2-8-2 5344 pulls freight through the Union Pacific transfer yard at Council Bluffs, Iowa, in 1952. Built by Baldwin in the 1920s, the Burlington rostered hundreds of 2-8-2s—ungainly machines that were considered homely by train-watchers and railroaders alike. But they more than made up in utility for what they lacked in looks, and they remained in service until the very end of steam.
William Kratville

ABOVE
In the early 1940s, Illinois Central E6 4004 and a mate take the New Orleans-bound Panama Limited out of Central Station, Chicago. This colored trim design was one of the classics created for EMD locomotive buyers. The grassy area is Grant Park, which once bordered Lake Michigan. Illinois Central filled in this area to build Central Station and the related yard trackage seen here.
Illinois Central Photo, MARS

RIGHT
The last incarnation of the Hiawatha is exemplified in this view at Columbus, Wisconsin, in 1950. A skytop observation lounge car trails the Chicago-bound Morning Hiawatha as an A-B-A set of westbound FP7s are rolling the Afternoon Hiawatha. The Milwaukee Road tastefully honored the name and legend of the chieftain with a classy motif on its most prestigious trains.
Milwaukee Road photo, MARS

The differences in animation between steam and diesel locomotives are quite apparent in this 1963 scene at the Clyde roundhouse in Cicero, Illinois. The diesel, GP30 937, idles as O-5 class 4-8-4 5632 passes by to prepare for an August 23 excursion for schoolkids. In the early morning light, the steam hissing from the open cylinder cocks and smoke plume heading for the heavens creates an image hard to match with diesels. The Burlington steam program helped bring the sights and sounds of steam to a generation born just too late.
Jim Boyd

During its first few months of operation Amtrak did not change the appearance of passenger trains very much from the predecessor railroads. Looking exactly like a Milwaukee Road train, this scene at Chicago Union Station shows a pair of E9s on one of the Hiawathas. The colors are those of the Union Pacific passenger trains, since this equipment continued through to the West Coast over Union Pacific rails. A notable omission is the Railway Post Office car. Passenger train losses soared with the loss of the railway mail shipments in the 1960s.
Jim Boyd

One of the railroads that called at St. Louis Union Station was the Frisco, a railroad that named its fleet of twenty-three crimson E-units for famous horses. Frisco E8s 2006, Traveller, and 2015, Twenty Grand, are backing a train into the terminal in June 1965. Locomotives that were repainted in 1965 or later lost the names under the cab window. Trains did not merely show up at St. Louis, they arrived, as the mouth of the station trackage had a vast two-track wye. Trains would back into the huge thirty-two-track trainshed observation-car first, if the train had one.
Jim Boyd

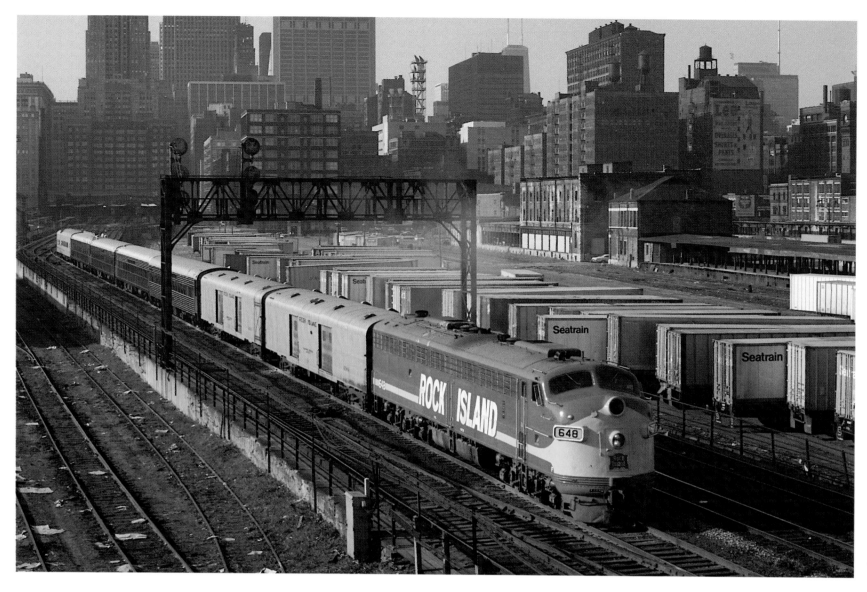

ABOVE
In a shiny fresh coat of red and yellow, Rock Island E8 648 has a short train in tow out of LaSalle Street Station, Chicago, in May 1970. The struggling and bankrupt Rock Island provided a fascinating show of vintage diesels in many color schemes during the 1970s. The 648 represents the Rock's last fling with its traditional red, before starting afresh with a light-blue-and-white Rock image. Ultimately, the road failed. Its equipment was sold and most of its vast expanse of trackage was either torn up or sold to other railroads.
Jim Boyd

RIGHT
A rare Milwaukee Road SDL39 leads an SD9 across the prairie at Hettinger, North Dakota, in October 1971. To supplement the Milwaukee's ageing six-axle EMD and Alco road switchers used on its prairie lines, EMD designed a lightweight version of the 2300hp turbo-charged SD39 riding on a short wheelbase version of the three-axle flexicoil truck. Never duplicated for another railroad, the SDL39s continue to work for regional railroad Wisconsin Central today.
Jim Boyd

Ash Street Tower in Chicago was a busy place: the parallel Santa Fe main line and the Illinois Central crossed, at grade, the tracks of the Baltimore & Ohio Chicago Terminal, the Chicago River & Indiana and the Pittsburgh, Cincinnati, Chicago & St. Louis; it is called "the Panhandle". The date is July 1971, and Amtrak is in its third month of existence as seven F-units wheel the Southwest Chief across the diamonds. Note that the ancient initials on the tower have the B&OCT letters in the wrong order.
Jim Boyd

LEFT

Highlands Station in Hinsdale, Illinois, is no stranger to fast passenger trains. The three-track main line was nicknamed "The Raceway," since everything from Zephyrs to commuter trains would race through this territory at high speeds. The former Chicago, Burlington & Quincy main line became part of the Burlington Northern empire on March 2, 1970. On May 1, 1971 BN turned over its passenger services to Amtrak. In this July 1971 scene of a long-distance Zephyr, not much has yet changed.
Jim Boyd

LEFT

The Chicago & Illinois Midland is a busy coal hauler based in Springfield, Illinois. It serves the on-line Commonwealth Edison power plants at Powerton and Pawnee, and a transloader at Havana that dumps coal into the Illinois River barges for transport up-river. On September 9, 1987, a southbound train of covered hoppers and boxcars was passing the former depot at Manito en route to Springfield.

Author photo

ABOVE

Three Frisco 3600hp SD45s lead a train past a grain elevator in Springfield, Missouri. It is May 1980, a year before Frisco was integrated into the Burlington Northern. A fast freight line, Frisco connected Birmingham with Kansas City and St. Louis with western Texas. Its location permitted it to participate in run-through freight from northeast to southwest with the Santa Fe and from southeast to northwest with Union Pacific and the Seaboard Coast Line.

Jim Boyd

RIGHT
One of Amtrak's Illinois Zephyr commuter trains rolls out of Chicago Union Station, passing the coach yard on September 21, 1990, at the beginning of a Friday afternoon rush hour. Nearly twenty years old, Amtrak during this era was a world-class railroad, with a unified look to all of its equipment. Soon Amtrak would begin replacing the stalwart F40s with brand new and rebuilt motive power in four different liveries, thus confusing its image for many years.
Doug Koontz

EVERYWHERE WEST & TEXAS

The region between the Missouri River and the front range of the Rocky Mountains is vast. The famous lyric, "amber waves of grain," is an apt description. Any ease of building through this territory was more than made up for by the miles of track a railroad had to build to cross it. After the American Civil War, railroads had reached the Kansas towns of Dodge City, Topeka and Wichita. Post-war shortages created a big demand for beef in Chicago and in the east, while Texas had plenty of long-horn cattle but no railroads to transport them. Driving large herds of long-horns overland north to the Kansas railheads began the era of the American cowboy. Soon, cattle drives were common, traversing routes known as the Santa Fe Trail and the Chisholm Trail. In less than twenty years, however, the invention of barbed wire would fence off the plains to cattle drives; and the coming of railroads to Texas would render them unnecessary anyway. The era of the cowboy ended in the 1880s. But the trails of the cattle drives and the wagon trains were soon followed by railroads, and today Union Pacific and the Burlington Northern Santa Fe haul record tonnage over these ancient routes.

EVERYWHERE WEST & TEXAS

For years the Missouri River defined America's western frontier. At St. Joseph, Missouri, in 1860, just forty miles upstream from Kansas City, the Pony Express began transporting mail and messages to and from California at the speed of a running horse. In only eighteen months, the constant relay of riders passed into history. At Omaha nearly 150 miles upstream and twelve years later, a railroad was created with the stroke of President Lincoln's quill on the Pacific Railroad Act of 1862. This road was the Union Pacific. Armed with land grants and creative capitalists, Union Pacific laid its first rails along the Missouri on July 10, 1865. It built west along the Platte River to make its legendary meeting, on May 10, 1869, with the Central Pacific at Promontory. In the coming years seven other railroads, and two in Canada, would span the same territory to connect and compete for east-west traffic.

Union Pacific struggled through the rest of the 1800s until Wall Streeter Edward H. Harriman gained control. Harriman raised money and developed Union Pacific into one of the strongest railroads in North America. In the 1980s and 1990s, it strategically acquired other railroads, and it is today the biggest of the big. Its original transcontinental main line from Omaha to Cheyenne handles more than ninety trains per day. Almost 130 years after it was formed, Union Pacific purchased its ancient rival, Southern Pacific.

The railroads bought by Union Pacific since the 1980s include the Missouri-Kansas-Texas, the Missouri Pacific, the Western Pacific, the Chicago & North Western and the Denver & Rio Grande— the latter was the parent company of Southern Pacific at the time of purchase. The Union Pacific today stretches west from Chicago, St. Louis, Memphis and New Orleans to every major shipping city on the Pacific coast.

While some teething problems from the Southern Pacific merger embarrassed Union Pacific managers, the corporation is financially strong enough to build or buy whatever it needs to correct any shortcomings, and it will. Union Pacific remains the only major railroad in America not to have changed its original name. More than any other company, Union Pacific is "America's Railroad."

Rivaling Union Pacific today is the Burlington Northern & Santa Fe. Number two in track miles, Burlington Northern & Santa Fe is also steeped in history and acquisitions. It was formed in 1995 when Burlington Northern bought Santa

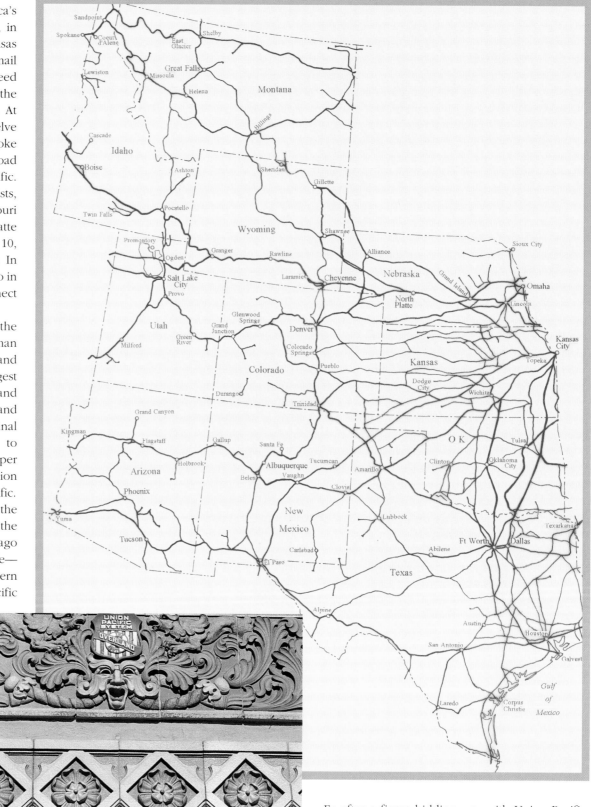

ABOVE

Elegant carvings and castings adorned many railroad stations. This one is on the restored Union Pacific depot in Marysville, Kansas.
Bob Gallegos

Fe after a fierce bidding war with Union Pacific. Burlington Northern & Santa Fe (BNSF) is perhaps best understood if we work backward.

The Atchison, Topeka & Santa Fe stretched from Chicago to Los Angeles, and extended its service to the San Francisco bay area. Santa Fe

PRINCIPAL OPERATORS

Atchison, Topeka & Santa Fe (BNSF)
Chicago, Burlington & Quincy (BNSF)
Chicago, Rock Island & Pacific

Denver & Rio Grande Western (UP)
Great Northern (BNSF)
Kansas City Southern

Milwaukee Road (Soo/CPR)
Missouri Pacific (UP)
Missouri-Kansas-Texas (UP)
Northern Pacific (BNSF)
Southern Pacific (UP)
St. Louis, San Francisco, the Frisco (BNSF)
St. Louis Southwestern, the Cotton Belt (UP)

Texas & Pacific (UP)

Western Pacific (UP)
Union Pacific

CONTEMPORARY OPERATORS

Amtrak
Burlington Northern Santa Fe
Kansas City Southern
Union Pacific
South Orient

(MODERN MERGED IDENTITIES ARE IN PARENTHESES)

LEFT
Almost invisible among the mesas of northern Arizona is the Canyon Diablo, which the Atchison, Topeka & Santa Fe had to bridge to reach Flagstaff and California. Just miles from the Arizona Divide, near a small town called Two Guns, a westbound Santa Fe train poses in the 1880s atop the spindly structure spanning the deep gorge.
Santa Fe photo, MARS

was and is known for rolling freight fast, and it developed a stable of steam power admired by most other railroads. It dieselized early, and was moving most of its freight with EMD model FTs before World War II. Passenger trains rolled behind streamlined diesels dressed in a stunning silver and red "war bonnet" paint scheme. Partially due to the Lionel toy trains running around post-World War II Christmas trees, that design would become the most recognized in railroading.

Santa Fe, as mentioned, was synonymous with fast freight, and even today BNSF maintains the fastest schedule between Chicago and the West Coast. Santa Fe had hinted at a coast-to-coast merger with the Erie Lackawanna in the 1970s. However, interest from the Southern Pacific diverted that energy with the forming of Southern Pacific Santa Fe in the 1980s. Certain of government approval, the corporations merged all subsidiaries except the railroad, though both roads painted locomotives in a new design. The Interstate Commerce Commission denied the merger, and the Santa Fe had to divest itself of the railroad, though it kept the non-rail holdings. Southern Pacific limped on, finding Rio Grande as a buyer.

The Burlington Northern was the 1970 sum of Chicago, Burlington & Quincy, the Northern Pacific, the Great Northern, the Spokane, Portland & Seattle and the Frisco. This created a huge system that connected the Pacific northwest with the Gulf of Mexico at Pensacola. The Northern Pacific and Great Northern were created by James J. Hill, who built main lines west from Minneapolis through Minnesota and Idaho to reach the ports of Seattle and Tacoma, Washington.

Milwaukee Road built its Pacific Extension west from the Twin Cities across Big Sky country to

compete directly with Great Northern and Northern Pacific. Milwaukee was well engineered, and since its owners also had interests in the copper industry the mountain passes were electrified. By the 1970s the line was abandoned.

The Chicago, Rock Island & Pacific was a strong company that built from Chicago westward, joining the Southern Pacific at Tucumcari. Its "Rockets" and Golden State Limited passenger trains were among the finest, but it had too much prairie trackage and had to file for bankruptcy in 1980.

A recent renegade in the region has been Kansas City Southern (KCS). Its roots date to 1890 when promoter Arthur Stillwell built the shortest rail route from Kansas City south to the Gulf of Mexico, at Port Arthur, also built by Stillwell. The discovery of oil in Texas bode well for Kansas City Southern, and in 1928 it merged with the east-west Louisiana & Arkansas Railway to get closer to Dallas. KCS is another of the old-order Class 1 railroads. While the larger railroads were merging around it in the 1990s, its president Mike Haverty made a bold move by purchasing a line directly to Mexico City. Using trackage rights over Union Pacific and the Texas-Mexican Railway, Kansas City Southern provides Mexico City with direct connections to Canada and Detroit's auto-makers. Haverty's Kansas City Southern stands to become a powerhouse of railroading.

The area west and south of the Missouri River today hosts more freight tonnage than any other part of the country. From the Powder River Basin of central Wyoming to Union Pacific's main line through Nebraska, or SP's Sunset Route through New Mexico and Arizona, or along the Santa Fe all the way along the old Route 66, train-watchers always leave rewarded with high-density action.

RIGHT
It is 1887 and the
construction crews are
building the St. Paul,
Minneapolis & Manitoba
Railway across the
badlands in the Dakota
territories. The special
"sky-scraper" cars were
used as dormitories for
the men out in the field,
and the soldiers on board
protected the workmen
from hostile Indian
attacks. The St.PM&M
would eventually become
the Great Northern, led
by Empire Builder James
J. Hill.
Burlington Northern photo,
Salamander Picture Library

LEFT
A stereoview image of a
Southern Pacific 4-4-0
No.81 in Yuma, Arizona,
during August 1877. This
is one of the locomotives
used to build SP's Sunset
Route across the deserts
of Arizona and New
Mexico. The balloon-
shaped, safety smoke
stacks were typical on
woodburning
locomotives.
MARS

ABOVE, INSET
June 3, 1887, at Hebron,
Nebraska, and this is the
first corn and grain train
rolling along the Chicago,
Rock Island & Pacific.
Rock Island photo,
Salamander Picture Library

LEFT
St.Paul, Minneapolis &
Manitoba Railway crews
in 1887 lay and spike rail
while trying to keep up
with the tie gangs.
Great Northern Railway,
MARS

LEFT
This 1898 view of a Union Pacific caboose shows it rather early in the concept's evolution, when railroads were still learning how to use them and protect its occupants. Note the ball signals hanging from the roof, and the number of chimneys surrounding the cupola. The small box near the cupola window was a house for a signal marker; on many roads that would be red if the caboose was on the main line, or green if it was on a siding. This would help engineers determine whether the caboose was fouling the main line.
UP Collection, Salamander Picture Library

BELOW
Missouri Pacific operated an extensive system that connected St. Louis and Omaha with New Orleans and the Texas coast and nearly every city in between. Passenger service was available over much of its system throughout the steam era. When purchased before World War I, 4-6-2s such as the 6509 here were the premier motive power for passenger trains. By the time this photo was taken, it had been replaced by 4-8-2s and 4-8-4s, but was still handling passengers admirably on the branch and secondary lines.
MP photo, MARS

LEFT
Under control of E.H. Harriman, the Union Pacific was a lean and mean railroad machine that standardized designs and made the most of its equipment. This 4-4-0 No.609 pulls out of Nebraska in 1912 with a short passenger train after having taken coal. The 4-4-0 was a relic even then, having been built in the 1880s but modernized with air brakes and electric lights. While 2-8-2s and 4-6-2s were being purchased for the main lines, vintage locomotives such as this were the main stay of the branch lines.
Union Pacific Collection

RIGHT
The Roaring Twenties were coming to an end when this photo of a Great Northern S-1 class 4-8-4 was made in 1929. Six of these were built by Baldwin for the GN in 1929, with seventy-three-inch driving wheels. Great Northern was another of the few North American railroads to favor the bellpaire firebox. While the GN ordered fourteen bigger 4-8-4s the following year with eighty-inch drivers, the earlier S-1s were more versatile in their ability to pull both freight and passenger trains over GN's modest grades.
Peter Newark's American Pictures

Southern Pacific shaved nearly 100 miles off its original transcontinental main line in 1903 by building a twenty-mile-long wooden trestle across the middle of the Great Salt Lake in Utah. The high cost of maintaining the bridge made it cheaper to replace it with a more stable dirt-fill. This publicity photo was taken on the Lucin Cutoff in the 1930s and shows the westbound Overland Limited passing another Southern Pacific train pulled by Southern Pacific 2461, a P-8 class 4-6-2 built by Baldwin in 1921. *Union Pacific Collection*

LEFT

Union Pacific was a pioneer of dieselization when it introduced two streamliner trainsets. In this 1934 photo, the M10001 is shown on its first run, climbing the grade out of Omaha, Nebraska. The M10000 was built slightly earlier, in 1934. These lightweight streamliners featured all-aluminum carbodies and an articulated design. The M10000 was named City of Salina, and the M10001 City of Portland.
Union Pacific Collection

RIGHT

The aluminum streamliners were capable of 110mph for great stretches, but to cover the schedules when they were being serviced the Union Pacific used this high-drivered streamlined 4-6-2. The styling on the 2906 was done by UP staff assistant Wayne Owens specifically to resemble the design of the M10000. The Union Pacific streamliners were among the best-looking in the land.
Union Pacific Museum Collection

LEFT

Santa Fe 3462 is brand new and quite stately in her appearance in this 1937 view. The second of five massive 4-6-4s from Baldwin, 3462's only peers were on the Milwaukee Road and Chicago & North Western, which rostered similar-sized speedsters. *Baldwin photo, Salamander Picture Library Collection*

BELOW

The Rock Island used stainless steel rolling stock and EMD E-series diesels on its famous Rocket series of streamliners. This is the Rocky Mountain Rocket, a sleek-nosed E6, during the late-1930s. *Rock Island photo, author collection*

RIGHT

Northern Pacific A-class 4-8-4 No.2611 leads a thirteen-car passenger train through the tiny town of De Smet, Montana, west of Missoula, on November 12, 1939. The dozen members of NP's 2600-series were very significant as the first order of 4-8-4s built for any railroad in the world, by the American Locomotive Company in 1926 and 1927. The 4-8-4 would become the most successful passenger and dual-service design, one that kept many railroads away from the maintenance-intensive articulateds. *AAR photo, MARS*

RIGHT
Union Pacific has hauled automobiles for as long as there have been any to haul. Three long strings of automobile boxcars representing three generations of design can be seen in this view from the mid-1940s at Omaha, Nebraska. Coupled to the locomotive are fifty-foot wooden cars built during the 1920s; the far string are steel cars with raised roofs to accommodate the loading of autos; and the middle string are new cars built for autos. The DS1300 was the first Fairbanks-Morse locomotive on Union Pacific roster, delivered during May 1945.
Author collection

LEFT
The Northern Pacific was burdened with treacherous grades in the Rocky Mountains in Montana. Here we see a westbound NP freight train wrestling with Bozeman Pass west of Livingston during March 1941. Northern Pacific employed 4-6-6-4s as pushers on Bozeman and Mullan passes, to help heavy trains over the 2 per cent grades. These hills were one of the proving grounds for EMD's FT 103 diesel set, which led to Northern Pacific purchasing several sets.
Northern Pacific photo, author collection

RIGHT

The morning sun glints off a Rio Grande Ski Train as its 4-8-4 climbs the Front Range of the Rockies at Fire Clay, Colorado, on December 26, 1949. The Denver & Rio Grande operated Ski Trains from Denver west to Winter Park, located at the west portal of the Moffat Tunnel.

Robert W. Andrews, author collection

BELOW

With his valve gear in full forward, the engineer is accelerating his Santa Fe 4-8-4 2921 through New Mexico with a freight train in tow during the late-1940s. These 1944 Baldwins were among the most respected 4-8-4s in the land, capable of 2,000-mile jaunts without an engine change.

Santa Fe photo, MARS

ABOVE

The Overland Limited sails westward through Echo Canyon, Utah, during the late-1940s. A 4-8-2 on this train was not uncommon when motive power was in short supply. The Overland Limited was one of UP's many fine passenger trains between Omaha and the West Coast. By the 1950s these runs were entirely pulled by diesels.

Union Pacific Collection

ABOVE AND LEFT
Observation lounge cars
(above) on Northern
Pacific's North Coast
Limited showed how
comfortable rail travel
had become by the late-
1940s. "Vista Domes" on
the North Coast Limited
(left) were different still;
the seats reclined but
were not reserved,
allowing passengers to
visit then return to their
seat.
*Burlington Northern photo,
MARS*

RIGHT
A steam-powered Empire
Builder approaches the
Continental Divide as it
crests Marias Pass in
northern Montana.
Marias is noteworthy for
being the lowest railroad
crossing of the Rockies.
*Great Northern photo,
Salamander Picture Library*

ABOVE
Union Pacific had a tradition of operating the biggest machines on rails. Before the giant 4-12-2s and 4-8-8-4s were all retired, UP began receiving gas turbine locomotives in 1953 that were ultimately capable of 8500hp. Here in the 1950s, we see 4500hp "veranda turbine" No.73 leading a train through the separated tunnels and flyover in Echo Canyon, Utah.
Union Pacific Collection

RIGHT
The North Coast Limited passes by the crags and narrow confines of Bozeman Pass on its westbound journey through the Rockies in the 1950s. The North Coast Limited was the pride of the Northern Pacific, and its two-tone green paint scheme was styled by Raymond Loewy. Vista-dome cars were a highlight of the train, offering passengers splendid scenic views.
Northern Pacific photo, MARS

ABOVE

A pair of Union Pacific 4-8-8-4s relax between helper assignments at Laramie, Wyoming, in the late-1950s. The 4-8-8-4s are considered the largest steam locomotives ever built. The name "Big Boy" is said to have been chalked on the smoke box door by an employee at the Alco plant, and the name stuck. The twenty-five Big Boys ran primarily west of Cheyenne, over Sherman Hill, and in the Wasatch Mountains of Utah.
Jim Shaughnessy

RIGHT

The engine hostler at Laramie, Wyoming, looks over the valve gear and spring rigging of a 4-8-8-4 laying over between helper assignments in the late-1950s. The stiff grades of Sherman Hill lay between Cheyenne and Laramie. Big Boys based in Cheyenne as helpers would shove trains over Sherman and then wait at Laramie to push eastbound trains back to Cheyenne.
Jim Shaughnessy

Looking as if it were traveling at the speed of sound, this Rio Grande K-36 class 2-8-2 is churning its way at all of 30mph heading south from Alamosa to Antonito, Colorado. The engineer is calm and confident with the pipe train he has in tow, bound for Farmington, New Mexico, during June 1963. The movement of supplies for pipeline construction projects kept the narrow gauge hauling freight into the 1960s. Today, segments of the three-foot-gauge out of Durango and Chama operate with these very same locomotives, keeping the spirit of the narrow gauge alive for a new generation.
Jim Shaughnessy

LEFT
Santa Fe's warbonnet-painted passenger locomotives graced many trains passing through Kansas City, Missouri, with names like the Chief, the Super Chief and the El Capitan. They also pulled many unnamed trains. In August 1966 a typical A-B consist of F7s pulls a mid-afternoon train to California.
Jim Boyd

ABOVE
As the summer sun is rising on a July morning in 1968, a northbound Kansas City Southern streamliner, The Flying Crow, is sailing across the long trestle north of Texarkana near Whatley, Arkansas. This is quite an exotic locomotive consist, with a freight F7, F3B, F3A and an E8 pulling the posh passenger train.
Jim Boyd

LEFT
Two "Little Joe" electrics lead the diesels assigned to Milwaukee Road Train 264 up to the snowline of St. Paul Pass near Falcon, Idaho, in May 1974. Built by General Electric in 1947 for Russia and never delivered due to international post-World War II politics, these unique locomotives were nicknamed "Little Joes" by railroaders after the Communist leader Joseph Stalin. General Electric sold the units to two American railroads, the Milwaukee Road, which primarily used them as helpers over the electrified mountain passes, and the interurban Chicago, South Shore & South Bend in northern Illinois.
Ted Benson

ABOVE
A pair of Union Pacific's 6600hp DDA40X diesels team up with a 5000hp DD35 to bring an eastbound freight down Sherman Hill at Dale, Wyoming, in 1975. These massive locomotives were used system-wide, but were kept on the main lines.
Robert R. Bahrs

RIGHT
A quartet of rare Alco RSD4s and RSD5s claw a train of empty coal hoppers up toward Soldier Summit and to the mines near Martin, Utah, during September 1975. The Utah Railway is an independent coal hauler that dates back to 1914.
Robert R. Bahrs

ABOVE
A Denver & Rio Grande
freight train rolls down
out of the Front Range
against the setting sun
during 1989. All five
locomotives have their
dynamic brakes in the
eighth notch to keep the
speed under control.
Scott Snell

RIGHT
Rio Grande train 742 led
by SD50s 5500 and 5502
and SD40T-2 5396 bursts
from the east portal of
Colorado's Moffat Tunnel
in September 1984. Built
by David Moffat, the
tunnel enabled his
Denver & Salt Lake
Railroad to penetrate the
Rockies head-on.
*Reid McNaught, Jim Boyd
Collection*

CALIFORNIA & THE PACIFIC COAST

It can be said that the West Coast is America's supermarket. Almost everything needed in life is either grown, pumped, harvested or manufactured there. California's fertile valleys, such as the San Joaquin and the Napa, bear some of the finest produce in the land. The deserts of southwest and central California produce cement and gypsum for wallboard, industrial substances such as trona and borax are processed there, and crude oil is found in many areas. Northern California, Oregon and Washington are primarily logging country. The major coastal cities have large seaports for both the import and export of goods.

But the industrial age did not get to California easily. The Sierra Nevada and mountain chains to the south were formidable enough to challenge every western traveler until the coming of the aircraft. Innovative engineering was required to build a railroad over and through these mountains. The first of these was Judah's Donner Pass route, and at least six other railroads would build treacherous mountain passes in order to reach the coast. Stephens and Stampede in Washington are among the most spectacular, while Cajon, at the gateway to the Los Angeles basin, still tests the mettle of the most alert railroad crews.

CALIFORNIA & THE PACIFIC COAST

The land of milk and honey in America is California. Its perfect weather, rugged mountains, fertile valleys, and picturesque deserts made this land sought after and fought over for centuries. But the discovery of gold in 1849 began the events that brought California into statehood. After winning the war with Mexico, the US Government bought the land that included California, and the United States' "manifest destiny" was realized.

Railroads were being built in California as early as the 1850s, but the rails and equipment had to be shipped around South America from the East Coast. The Sierra Nevada and Rocky mountains seemed insurmountable at the time, but a surveyor named Theodore Judah had discovered a viable route through the former. He interested a group of San Francisco businessmen, then traveled to Washington to sell the idea to the US Congress. Judah died of an illness contracted during his traveling between the coasts, but the railroad got built over Donner Pass. It stretched through Nevada and around the Great Salt Lake to that famous meeting at Promontory Point in 1869.

What was then the Central Pacific Railroad was gradually becoming the Southern Pacific by the mid-1880s. The Southern Pacific was building from Sacramento south to Los Angeles, and then eastward into Texas. (The reason for the new company was to ease and delay the profit-based repayment of the government loans to build the Central Pacific.) Southern Pacific in the nineteenth century was driven by Collis P. Huntington, one of Central Pacific's four founders. Huntington also owned the Chesapeake & Ohio and other railroad interests, which he controlled from New York City. When Huntington died in 1900, Edward H. Harriman bought Huntington's Southern Pacific stock from the estate. Harriman had already engineered the financial rebirth of the Union Pacific, and by 1907 he was in control of the Union Pacific, Southern Pacific, Illinois Central, Oregon Short Line, Oregon Railway & Navigation and the Los Angeles & Salt Lake. Harriman was a master of financing, and he re-engineered and rebuilt much of the original Southern Pacific and Union Pacific. But he suffered from "bigness." Pressured about a western rail monopoly, President Roosevelt ordered Harriman to divest of his Southern Pacific stock. The Southern Pacific and Union Pacific were competitors again, but that would change nearly ninety years later when Union Pacific would again buy Southern Pacific—with Government blessing, of course.

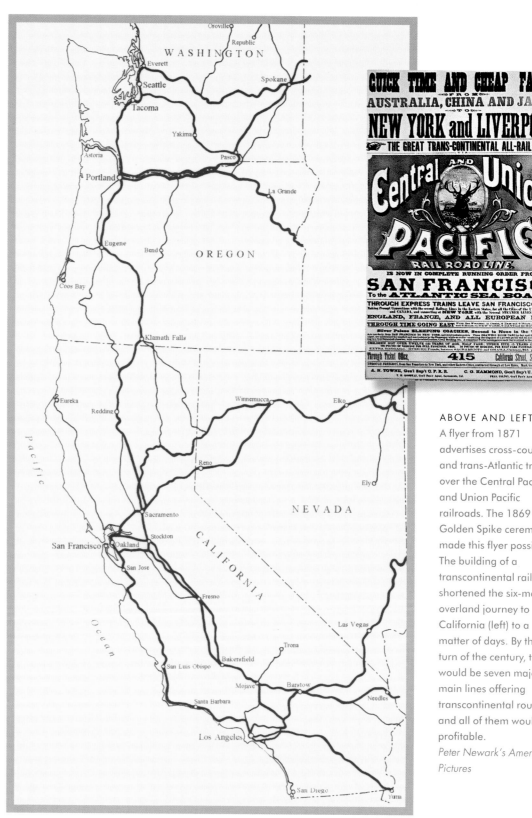

By 1900 the ports of Portland, Oregon, and Seattle and Tacoma, Washington, were served by Harriman's Union Pacific, and by James J. Hill's Northern Pacific and Great Northern. To bring the latter's traffic to Portland from Spokane without running over Harriman's Oregon Railway & Navigation, Hill built the Spokane, Portland & Seattle. Completed in 1909, this line was well engineered: trains rolled over several lofty bridges and through many tunnels and cuts.

PRINCIPAL OPERATORS

Atchison, Topeka & Santa Fe (BNSF)
Great Northern (BNSF)

Northern Pacific (BNSF)
Milwaukee Road

Southern Pacific (UP)
Spokane, Portland & Seattle (BNSF)

Union Pacific
Western Pacific (UP)

CONTEMPORARY OPERATORS

Amtrak
Burlington Northern Santa Fe
Caltrans
Union Pacific

(MODERN MERGED IDENTITIES ARE IN PARENTHESES)

Another late-coming transcontinental was the Western Pacific (WP). Its main financier was George Gould, son of Jay, who wanted a railroad to bring traffic from his Denver & Rio Grande to California. While it would parallel the Southern Pacific most of the way across Nevada to reach Salt Lake City, WP had to build through the Feather River Canyon. Such an idea had many critics. Undaunted, Gould built it and the first train rolled through on August 21, 1910.

Western Pacific had the easiest grade of all the transcontinentals, but money did not come as easily. It was first bankrupt in 1916, and again in 1935 during the Great Depression. Still, financial hardships created a strong employee loyalty. By the 1950s it was a leader, with its own luxury passenger train and state-of-the-art signaling. It was a railfan favorite throughout its history, but on December 22, 1982, the Western Pacific became part of Union Pacific. Harriman's successors didn't kill the Western Pacific, they poured much-needed capital into the Feather River Canyon, and it remains a vital route that complements nearby Donner Pass, now also operated by Union Pacific.

Hill did not miss an opportunity to irritate Harriman. He built south from Oregon to reach the Western Pacific, while the Western Pacific was building north from Keddie to meet Hill in an effort to bring the Great Northern into the Bay Area. Meanwhile, the Southern Pacific was building its Natron Cut-Off, later called the Cascade Line, north from the Bay Area into Portland as a short cut to the serpentine Siskiyou Line. Both were completed in the mid-1920s.

Southern Pacific's steam era was spectacular. The streamliner years were kind to the passenger locomotives and several 4-8-4s, 4-8-2s and a few 4-6-2s wore vivid orange and red skirts for the famous Daylight series of passenger trains. For its road freight locomotives, Southern Pacific built powerful, oil-fired articulateds with the cab in the front, to relieve crews of the hellish exhaust while passing through its many tunnels and snow sheds. Known as "cab forwards," they were unique to Southern Pacific. The Daylight's colors were even more striking on Southern Pacific's diesel fleet, while the freight diesels got a simpler black with orange and silver "black widow" image.

Union Pacific, through its purchase of Southern Pacific in 1997 and the Western Pacific in 1982, is now the dominant railroad in California. While the Santa Fe had a big presence in Los Angeles and San Diego, and its own tracks north to the Bay Area, a condition of the UP-SP merger in 1997 was that Burlington Northern & Santa Fe got access to the major ports. Union Pacific gets the same at the Burlington Northern & Santa Fe ports.

Meanwhile, in the 1980s and 1990s, the West Coast rediscovered commuter rail. While San Francisco never gave up on it, Los Angeles, and one by one the major western cities are entering the "commute" business, and operations are expanding onto previously freight-only tracks. Washington State purchased three Talgo trainsets that Amtrak is operating between Seattle, Washington, and Vancouver, British Columbia, as the Mount Baker International. West Coast railroading is alive and well.

BELOW
Union Pacific 4-4-0 934 is in the charge of a fruit block full of California produce circa 1890. These boxcars were well-insulated enough to keep the fruit in good condition for the journey, but such trains were still given priority during the harvest season to hasten the trip. The staff-mounted brake wheels are a reminder of when brakemen rode the tops of such cars. Brakemen were required to apply the brakes on up to five cars per man upon the whistle command from the locomotive engineer.
Union Pacific , J.G Moore Collection

RIGHT
This is Rockland, California, on the original transcontinental main line a little east of Sacramento around 1890, as the crew from Central Pacific 4-6-0 No.82 poses for a portrait with an early caboose. The venerable little Ten-Wheeler was built in 1868 by the Rogers Locomotive Works of Paterson, New Jersey.
Southern Pacific photo, MARS

ABOVE

The rotary snowplow enabled the railroads to remove deep snow that would normally stall the biggest of locomotives. This 1890s view shows Southern Pacific rotary No.2 fighting snow in the Sierra Nevada mountains on the main line near Donner Pass. Snowfall can accumulate to twenty or thirty feet during a typical season on Donner summit, named for a wagon train stranded in snow there before the railroad was built.
AAR photo, Salamander Picture Library

RIGHT

Hood River, Oregon, was a busy railroad town at the turn of the century. Located at the confluence of the Hood River and the Columbia, the town boasted a large Union Pacific depot near the junction of the Hood River Railroad and the UP main line. Here, a UP passenger train departs eastward after making its station stop.
Union Pacific Collection

The Western Pacific was the last of the big roads to reach California. Its first train finally rolled through the Feather River Canyon in August 1910: a burly 2-8-0 No.1, built by Baldwin in 1906.
AAR photo, Salamander Picture Library

The distinctive Pillars of Hercules are located along the Columbia River between Washington and Oregon. This is a Spokane, Portland & Seattle train in 1910.
Union Pacific Collection, Salamander Picture Library

ABOVE

In good weather, the observation platform was the best seat in the house for train travel. And what better train than the Sunset Limited, Southern Pacific's posh connection between New Orleans and Los Angeles? In 1910, when this photo was made, the trip took three days and three nights.

Salamander Picture Library

LEFT
The *Contra Costa* was the largest car ferry in the Southern Pacific fleet; it could transfer two locomotives and twenty-four passenger cars, or thirty-six freight cars. The ferry entered service in 1914 but was retired in 1930, when SP constructed a massive bridge across the Carquinez Straits.
AAR photo, Salamander Picture Library

BELOW
Among the many problems of steam railroading were the line-side fires caused by hot coals and exhaust sparks. This Southern Pacific firefighter outfit from the 1920s is putting out a fire in the Sierra Nevada mountains undoubtably set by one of SP's massive pushers.
Union Pacific Collection

In this 1927 scene at Riverside, California, a band of troubadours are serenading the observation car passengers on Union Pacific's Los Angeles Limited. Railroads often planned fanfare around its finer trains to attract publicity and ridership. The Los Angeles Limited was UP's crack train between Chicago and Los Angeles.
Salamander Picture Library

Union Pacific 4-8-2 No.7853 is in charge of the Los Angeles Limited on this day in 1929 as it splits the semaphores near Riverside, California. The Los Angeles Limited, the pride of the UP, boasted an all-Pullman consist before and during the Great Depression. The train established a clientele of movie personalities during the 1930s, and seldom was the train not full. The arch roofed Harriman-styled baggage car adds a distinct UP flavor to the heavyweight Pullmans.
Don H. Roberts photo, Union Pacific Collection

LEFT
Railroad shopmen were a significant class of skilled labor on the railroads. In the 1920s, more than 420,000 people were employed by the US rail system purely to maintain freight cars and locomotives. In August 1931 a team of ten men attack a Northern Pacific refrigerator car to return it to interchange service. During this era, many such cars were painted in bold colors and lettering, this one advertising the apples from the Yakima Valley of Washington State.
Minnesota Historical Society, Salamander Picture Library

ABOVE
Many railroads outfitted freight gondolas with chairs and railings to accommodate passengers on special excursions. These made the best observation cars, and they normally traveled at the rear of a train. Southern Pacific gondola 2806 was so equipped for special train service, and it is shown in 1930 on an excursion as it skirts Odell Lake in Oregon.
Union Pacific Collection

LEFT

A nose view of Southern Pacific 4-8-4 4412 shows the sleek styling of these massive locomotives. Built by Lima Locomotive Works in 1936, the GS-2 was designed in-house by SP shop employees. With eight eighty-inch driving wheels, the GS-series 4-8-4s were capable of ninety mph with ease and were used on SP's new Daylight service.

Salamander Picture Library

ABOVE

The observation car on the Daylights was nearly as stunning as the locomotive. These fluted cars followed the GS-2s, -3s, and -4s everywhere they went, and they featured the same red-and-orange with silver trimming color scheme. Here, one of the cars is about to depart from Los Angeles Union Passenger Terminal in 1941.

AAR photo, Salamander Picture Library

LEFT

The equestrian-themed bar in the Union Pacific lounge car Little Nugget reflects America's tastes in interior decoration just prior to World War II. Parlor cars such as this were works of art, with hand-carved trim and finishing. Note the genuine cuspidor on the floor.

Union Pacific Collection

ABOVE

Stevedores unload automobiles from boxcars in Portland, Oregon, during May 1953 at the Portland Traction Company's loading dock. Since before World War I, boxcars had been the most efficient method of shipping automobiles, which were driven into the cars and onto racks that inclined to permit more efficient loading. Normally six autos could fit into a single boxcar. The Santa Fe boxcars to the right were rebuilt from wooden cars made by the US Government for the Santa Fe during World War I.

Riley W. Dunam, author collection

RIGHT

Immediately after the United States had joined World War II, the troop trains began to roll. Here we see a company of Royal Air Force men from Great Britain in southern California during December 1941, having just arrived on a Union Pacific train from the east. Troop trains moved many millions of servicemen during the four years of the war. At some depots, "canteens" were set up by local families to provide coffee and meals to military personnel; the best known of these was at North Platte, Nebraska.

Union Pacific Collection

ABOVE

Santa Fe 4-8-4 3775 gets a roll on as it bites into the grades of Cajon Pass just east of San Bernardino, California. The train is the Grand Canyon Limited, and it has just overtaken a freight train on the siding at Devore, at the foot of the grade. The Santa Fe built a sixty-mile branch from its main line to the South Rim of the canyon, and it helped develop the National Park there.
AT&SF photo, MARS

RIGHT

The crew of a UP articulated locomotive gets a friendly wave from the hind-end brakeman as it leads a freight train through Meacham, Oregon, in the heart of the Blue Mountains in 1948. The UP main line is a tough piece of railroad that tests the mettle of locomotives and crews alike. In the mid-1990s UP began double-tracking most of it for smoother operation.
Union Pacific Collection

ABOVE

The date is January 23, 1955, and the brakemen of the daily Sierra Railroad freight train are walking on the tops of moving freight cars to apply the brakes. The train is rolling gently through Keystone, California, before it begins the steep descent into Cooperstown.
Al Rose

RIGHT

A typical cafe lounge car during the 1950s. Partitioned into three functional sections, the cars feature a lounge room with seating for sixteen people, a snack bar and restaurant-style counter with stools. This car is part of the Union Pacific fleet.
AAR photo, Salamander Picture Library

BELOW
Edmonds, Washington, located seventeen miles north of Seattle along Puget Sound, was a conditional stop for all transcontinental and international trains of the Great Northern Railway. In this scene from the 1950s, the train has stopped to pick up passengers. To get a train to stop, the station would change the signal again on the roof of the depot so that the engineer would see and stop.
Great Northern photo, Salamander Picture Library

RIGHT
Northern Pacific's North Coast Limited leaves King Street Station in Seattle, Washington, as it begins its transcontinental trip eastward to Chicago. The streamliner covered the 1,900 miles between St. Paul and Seattle in thirty-six hours, passing through some of the finest Rocky Mountain scenery en route. Northern Pacific and Great Northern shared this depot in Seattle. The NP streamliners were normally filled with vacationers from the East Coast looking to spend their time away from home wallowing in Rocky Mountain scenery.
Northern Pacific photo

ABOVE

An A-B-B-B quartet of E9s lead the City of Portland in this Union Pacific publicity photo. The Armour yellow color scheme of Union Pacific is the oldest in continual use in all of railroading. It was introduced in 1934 (with a brown roof) on streamliner M10000, and it has personified the UP's diesel fleet ever since. UP once ran an extensive system of streamliners connecting Chicago, St. Louis, Kansas City, Portland, San Francisco and Los Angeles; today it maintains an A-B-A set of E9s to pull its business train.
Union Pacific Museum, MARS London Collection

RIGHT

The Great Northern and the Spokane, Portland & Seattle railroads both shared a grand stone station in Spokane, Washington. During July 1969, two Spokane, Portland & Seattle C425s lead a westbound freight past the downtown depot. At Spokane, the Portland sections of the Empire Builder and North Coast Limited, as well as Portland-bound Great Northern freight, were switched onto the SP&S. The 1970 Burlington Northern (BN) merger eliminated the need for the SP&S, and BN demolished the old facilities to provide a site for the 1974 World's Fair.
Jim Boyd

RIGHT

Western Pacific's famous California Zephyr heads east at Pulga, California, on its daily journey through the rugged Feather River Canyon. Built in Philadelphia by the Budd Company and jointly operated by the Burlington, the Rio Grande and the Western Pacific, the California Zephyr was perhaps the greatest "cruise train" in America. It raced across the prairies and deserts in darkness, and traversed the spectacularly scenic Rocky Mountains on the Rio Grande and the Feather River route of Western Pacific in daylight.
Jim Boyd

LEFT

The Sierra Railroad train order read "Extra Three East" for this November 1975 special trip with the company business car. While Ten-Wheeler No.3 is hardly winded with just one car in tow, it was vocal enough to motivate the cattle and the blackbirds near Montezuma, California. The Sierra Railroad has hosted many television and motion picture companies over the years, and No.3 seems to be Hollywood's favorite. The 4-6-0 was built in 1891 by the Rogers Locomotive Works in Paterson, New Jersey.
Ted Benson

ABOVE

In the summer of 1969, a C424, a C425, two FA1s and an RS3 lead a westbound Spokane, Portland & Seattle (SP&S) freight into Wishram, Washington, along the Columbia River. The Spokane, Portland & Seattle was a western anomaly, its freight service entrusted almost entirely to a fleet of Alco-built road switchers and cab units. The SP&S passenger trains, the Empire Builder and North Coast Limited that served Portland, Oregon, were powered by EMD diesels.
Jim Boyd

RIGHT

The morning sun is just over the hill tops in California gold rush country as the Sierra Railroad freight train rolls downgrade through the secluded curve on the railroad known as Canyon Tank. Between the distinctive Baldwin switcher and the caboose are five loaded woodchip hoppers from the mill at Chinese Camp. During the steam era, there was a water tank here in the Dry Creek Canyon, between Cooperstown and Keystone. Not far from Canyon Tank is Sutter's Mill, where gold was discovered in 1849.

Ted Benson

Westbound Southern Pacific freight travels compass-east into the dawn's early light as it crests the top of Cajon Pass at Summit, California, on March 12, 1989. The headquarters of Southern Pacific was in San Francisco, so to establish a system-wide sense of direction its timetables considered everything heading toward San Francisco as westbound. Cajon Pass is the gateway into and out of the Los Angeles basin. The pass is also shared by the Santa Fe and Union Pacific.

Author photo

San Bernardino, California, is a Santa Fe town that grew up at the foot of Cajon Pass. It was the location of a large steam back shop and car shops, all of which were closed during the 1990s. Here on Sunday evening, March 13, 1988, a westbound UP train is rolling into San Bernardino yard with the mountains of the same name as a backdrop. Southern Pacific negotiates over Cajon pass through San Bernardino on its own trackage east of here.

Author photo

LEFT
Deep in the hills of California gold rush country labors one of America's most famous short lines, the Sierra Railroad. The sight of two rare Baldwin S12 switchers coupled nose to nose while doing the day's works is almost a signature image of the 1970s and 1980s. On April 10, 1990, the Sierra Baldwins are laboring around a curve and upgrade through Sonora, California, en route to the lumber mill at Standard, the end of the line. Wooden trestles, once common, are becoming as rare as the Baldwins. New management retired the Baldwins later in the decade.
Author photo

OH, CANADA!

Transcontinental railroads are a way of life north of the border, as two railroads spanned Canada throughout most of the industrial age. Indeed, few countries in the world can boast that their very formation was due to the railroad. For British Columbia joined the Dominion in 1871 only on condition that a railroad be built to connect it to the rest of the nation within ten years. Canadian railroading is spectacular, and engineers had a tougher time building them than their counterparts in the United States. While American railroads used loops to keep grades moderate, Canadian Pacific had to build a loop within a mountain, called Spiral Tunnels, to ease the grade of Kicking Horse Pass.

The United States has several long tunnels, but in 1989 CP Rail opened the seven-mile Mount Macdonald tunnel through the Selkirks. The sights of CN and CPR clinging to the walls of the Fraser River Canyon in British Columbia are among the best in all of railroading. In today's world of the North American Free Trade Agreement (NAFTA) between Canada, the United States and Mexico, Canada's railroads have been adjusting. CPR has controlled the Soo Line and Delaware & Hudson for many years, and Canadian National in 1998 purchased Illinois Central to reach Gulf ports and the Mexican border.

LEFT
One of the classic scenes of railroading: a block operator keeping track of train movements. This is wartime along the Canadian National (CNR), as evidenced by the Vendor of War Savings Stamps sticker on the window and the passing CNR locomotive outside. This is certainly a posed scene, as rail photography during the war was considered espionage—also because the operator's desk is too uncluttered, and the hanging bulletins and notices are too neat!
Canadian National photo/MARS

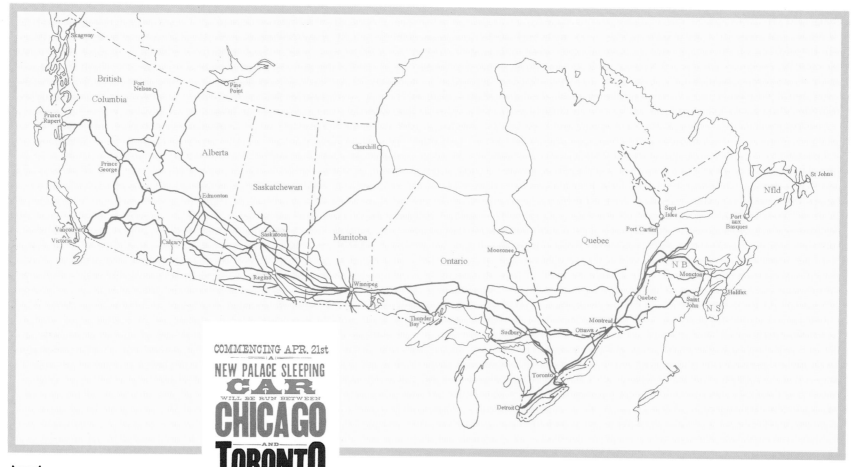

The history of railroading in Canada parallels that of the United States. But there are significant differences in the construction, corporate structure and operation. Topography is more extreme to the north, so the Canadians had a tougher time building roads across the continent. Complicated, lengthy tunnel projects, fewer mountain passes and the need to build over many miles of muskeg—the swampy, cold-climate version of the Everglades—were just a few of the engineering challenges. Two of Canada's big railroads operate their own main lines between the Atlantic and Pacific oceans. Both Canadian National and Canadian Pacific are true transcontinentals. The United States does not have a single high-tonnage main line spanning the entire continent, though the industry pundits believe the next round of mergers will create two or three such systems. In Canada, two cross-country railroads are a way of life. Indeed, the very nation was formed on the condition that the government build a railway.

Descriptions exist of modest horse-powered railways in Canada dating to 1830. However, Canada's first true railway was the Champlain & St. Lawrence. From a steamboat wharf in LaPairie, across the St. Lawrence River from the island of Montreal, a British-built 0-4-0 hauled two carriages with passengers more than fourteen miles east to St. Johns on the Richelieu River. The date was July 21, 1836, and this was Canada's first steam locomotive pulling its first train over its first railway. In the United States, the "firsts" all occurred on different railroads. The Champlain & St. Lawrence eventually built to the north end of Lake Champlain.

The railway bug had bitten, and railroad schemes surfaced all over Canada. Its second railway was a well-engineered coal hauler in Nova Scotia called the Albion Colliery Tramway, which opened in 1838 and purchased two British-built 0-6-0s. This remarkable little railway operated for fifty years, and afterward set aside its locomotives as historic relics. Both 0-6-0s are on display in Nova Scotia near where they operated.

Much as had been the case in the United States, the colonial government was initially more supportive of road and canal projects than railway construction. That changed. Canada's trackage increased from some 100 miles in 1851, to more than 2,000 miles a decade later. After the 1867 event known as Confederation, whereby the eastern provinces united with Quebec and Ontario to form the Dominion of Canada, the government sponsored a railway to connect this territory. By 1876 the Intercolonial Railway was completed. Prince Edward Island and Manitoba joined Canada in 1873. British Columbia had joined two years previously, on July 20, 1871, when Canada's first prime minister, Sir John A. Macdonald, had promised that a railroad would reach British Columbia within ten years.

The Canadian Pacific Railway began as a government effort. Ground broke first near Thunder Bay on June 1, 1875 (at this time the road was known as the Pacific Railway). Macdonald enthusiastically supported construction, and he enlisted contractors to build the various sections. Andrew Onderdonk from New York built the line from the Pacific eastward through Fraser River Canyon, while other crews worked westward from Montreal across the Precambrian Shield north of

RIGHT
Crews laying track in the lower Fraser River Valley of British Columbia in 1883, making good on Prime Minister Sir John A. Macdonald's promise to bring a railroad to British Columbia. By this time William Cornelius Van Horne was general manager of the Canadian Pacific Railway (CPR), and he was pushing the road to completion. Trains were running by 1886.
Canadian Pacific photo

PRINCIPAL OPERATORS

Algoma Central (WC)

Canadian Pacific Railway

Canadian National Railway
Northern Alberta Railway
Ontario Northland Railway
Pacific Great Eastern Railway (BCR)

CONTEMPORARY OPERATORS

Algoma Central
British Columbia Railway
Canadian Pacific Railway
Canadian National Railway
Northern Alberta Railway
Ontario Northland Railway
RaiLink Limited
VIA Rail

(MODERN MERGED IDENTITIES ARE IN PARENTHESES)

the Great Lakes, through the prairies and into the Rockies. Grading a right-of-way near the Great Lakes was arguably more difficult than crossing the Rockies, as the swampy muskeg would often swallow an entire locomotive—and the track on which it was sitting. On February 15, 1881, the House of Commons incorporated the Canadian Pacific Railway as a private corporation. In December of that year, William Cornelius Van Horne became its general manager, and he pushed the Canadian Pacific Railway to completion. The transcontinental Canadian Pacific Railway was completed in 1885, and cross-country trains were running by 1886.

As the Canadian Pacific Railway expanded and built new lines, other railroad companies began competing for routes and business. During the 1870s and 1880s, short lines were being built to serve the prairie farmers, and roads such as the Grand Trunk and Canadian Northern had completed lines to the Pacific. Traffic slumped after World War I and many of these independent companies were on the point of collapse. In 1917, control of the Canadian Northern passed to the government, as did control of the other railroads in the coming years. On December 20, 1918, this family of lines became known as the Canadian National Railways. Further amalgamations occurred, but by 1923 the Canadian main line rail scene was in place. The rail map remained generally unchanged until the 1990s; the private Canadian Pacific Railway was operating more than 23,000 miles of track, while the government-run Canadian National Railways was running more than 35,000 miles.

The finances and fortunes of the two Canadian

transcontinentals roughly paralleled those of America's larger railroads. The modern steam locomotives of the Canadian Pacific Railway and Canadian National Railways were based on American designs, though provincial laws required that the locomotives be manufactured in Canada, and this was a tradition continued into the diesel years.

Passenger rail travel all over North America had dwindled during the 1950s and 1960s as better highways were constructed. In 1974 the government formed VIA Rail Canada, and by 1978 VIA operated most of Canada's intercity passenger trains. Meanwhile, the larger cities developed commuter operations.

The 1990s would significantly change the Canadian rail map. Initially, the government permitted both big railroads to abandon marginal lines. Viable lines were sold to other operators; trackage that had no buyers was abandoned. The railroads on Prince Edward Island and Newfoundland were among those to go. Canadian Pacific extended its reach to the port cities of New York, Philadelphia and Baltimore with its 1990 purchase of the Delaware & Hudson.

In 1996 the government privatized Canadian National Railways in what was the largest public stock offering in history. As a private company, Canadian National's leader Paul Tellier has cut costs and improved efficiencies to the point where Canadian National is one of the strongest railroads in the world, perhaps eclipsing rival Canadian Pacific Railway. In 1998, Canadian National announced that it was buying Illinois Central, which would extend Canadian National's reach to New Orleans and Texas for access to Mexico.

LEFT
New Brunswick Ten-Wheeler No.40 poses with her crew at an unrecorded lumber yard during the late-1880s. During this era, the crew was usually assigned to a locomotive, and crews generally cared for it as if they owned it. Indeed, the first job of aspiring young railroaders was usually as an engine wiper. Even the tender extension, which allows the fuel to be stacked higher, has been painted and pin-striped.
TRH Pictures collection

BELOW
Snow has been a fierce rival of railroading since the first tracks were laid. In this late-1880s scene on Rogers Pass in British Columbia, it appears that the plow-equipped 2-8-0 No.402 has just replaced the passenger locomotive in the distance to get this train through the pass. Deep snow can stall the most powerful locomotives.
Boorne & May photo: Canadian Pacific, Salamander Picture Library

RIGHT
Canadian Pacific Railway No.1 poses with her full crew during the 1880s. While it may seem that this is CPR's first locomotive, in fact several contractors hired to build the original main line were known to have lettered locomotives as the No.1. This No.1 is believed to have been built in 1881 by the Portland Company in Oregon.
TRH Pictures collection

RIGHT
Canadian Pacific Railway 4-6-0 No.223 (an ST-3 class 4-6-0 with sixty-nine-inch drivers) was built in Canadian Pacific's own New Shops in Montreal in May of 1900. After a few renumberings, she was scrapped in 1929. The 4-6-0 was the next step in locomotive design after the 4-4-0 and the 4-4-2. The extra driving wheel increased tractive effort, and supported a larger boiler. The rounded corners near the cab indicate that the locomotive had a belpaire firebox, which provided a larger heating surface; this produced more steam than the conventional round firebox. The CPR was among the few roads that tried this design.
Canadian Pacific photo, TRH Pictures collection

RIGHT
Pictures from the turn of the century showing railroads in action are rare. In this scene, Canadian Pacific Railway 4-4-2 No.209 is speeding a passenger train from Montreal to Ottawa in 1900.
Canadian Pacific photo, TRH Pictures collection

BELOW
A Toronto, Hamilton & Buffalo train has made its station stop at Hamilton, Ontario, in 1900 and the station and baggage agents are transloading parcels and baggage. The elevated crossing shanty was once a common sight in North America. An employee in that shanty could watch for trains and oncoming auto or horse traffic. He would climb down the ladder to operate the crossing gates, and he would also set the order boards that would tell oncoming trains to stop.
Canadian Pacific photo, MARS

ABOVE
This scene from the Toronto, Hamilton & Buffalo in May 1905 shows the business side of the typical railroad station in a medium-sized city. It is these gentleman who would be contacted by telegraph or by messenger, and later by telephone, to discuss freight rates and loading options, the ordering of empty freight cars, or to check the status of an en-route shipment. The office would also handle the payroll for all the local railroad employees.
Canadian Pacific photo, MARS

LEFT
Toronto, Ontario, was a busy place before World War I, as this scene dated August 27, 1914, depicts. To the right are strings of ice-cooled refrigerated boxcars from the West Coast that hauled California produce to market. The raised hatches show that the ice compartments are empty, suggesting that the goods have already been unloaded and that the cars have been cleaned and are waiting for home-bound loads.
Alvin Smith collection

BELOW

Western Canada is arguably the most scenic region in North America, and its beauty has not changed with time. This scene from the 1920s shows one of Canadian Pacific's transcontinental passenger trains at Leanchoil, British Columbia, near Field. The locomotive is a D9-class 4-6-0, built by the American Locomotive Company in Schenectady, New York, in 1903.
Canadian Pacific photo, Salamander Picture Library

RIGHT

Before motorized trucks, freight was delivered to its final destination on wagons drawn by teams of horses. Driven by teamsters, the wagons were loaded and unloaded on sidings called "team tracks." This scene from 1919 shows Canadian National Express teamsters with live chickens that had just been unloaded from insulated express and baggage cars.
Canadian National photo, Salamander Picture Library

BELOW
The Great Depression of the 1930s hit all of North America hard, causing many to uproot and move to find a new life and a new start. In this scene along the Canadian Pacific Railway, these people are relocating from Montreal to Lois, British Columbia, during the 1930s. During this era, horses and sleds were the surest method of getting through the snow.
Salamander Picture Library

LEFT
The Canadian railroads were slow to adopt streamlined passenger equipment, but not so in streamlining locomotives. This illustration from 1936 shows Canadian National Railway 4-8-4 No. 6401 in full stride as it accelerates the Maple Leaf between Quebec and Toronto. The Maple Leaf continued on to New York City via Buffalo and the Lehigh Valley Railroad.
Peter Newark's American Pictures

Canadian National's popular U-class 4-8-4s were also in service on the CNR-owned Grand Trunk Western that connected Ontario with Detroit and Chicago. This scene in the early 1940s shows a workaday example near the Sarnia tunnels with US-bound reefers.
Canadian National photo

The roundhouse was the heart of any steam-era railroad. A rotating bridge with a building circling it was the most efficient way to store and maintain steam locomotives. Hundreds of roundhouses dotted the North American industrial landscape. This scene from the 1940s shows Canadian National's Turcot Roundhouse in Montreal, which was built with thirty stalls (it was later enlarged to a capacity of fifty-eight stalls). Contrary to popular belief, only running repairs and basic maintenance were performed at a roundhouse. All major work was done in the back shop.
Canadian National photo, MARS

Looking more like an office than a piece of rolling stock, this is the scene within a typical caboose; this one is on the Toronto, Hamilton & Buffalo railroad. The caboose was home to freight crews not required to ride in the locomotive. Most cabooses had a cupola: a raised area from which a brakeman could see his moving train.
Canadian Pacific photo, MARS

Even though the Grand Trunk Western was owned by the Canadian National, it still moved plenty of equipment for the United States military during World War II. The many automobile manufacturing plants located along the Grand Trunk had switched production to tanks for the war effort.
Canadian National photo

Canadian Pacific's main line through the Rockies is spectacular. In this 1947 view, we see one of CPR's legendary 2-10-4s, No.5926, pulling a heavyweight consist in the shadows of the Selkirk Mountains between Lake Louise and Banff, Alberta. The CPR bought these T-1s in 1938 and it named that wheel arrangement for the mountain range. The Selkirks were the largest streamlined steam locomotives in North America.
Canadian Pacific photo

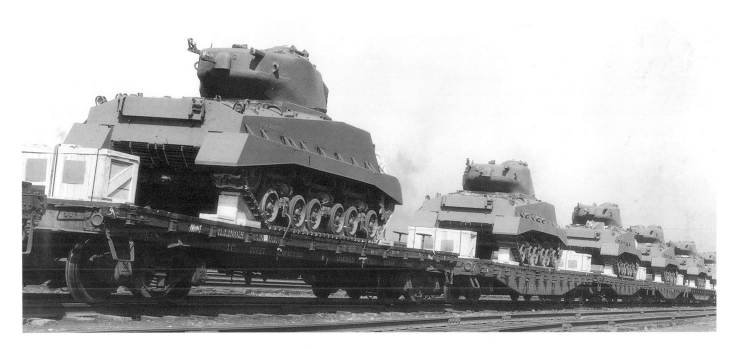

BELOW
Sherbooke, Quebec, was an important junction ninety-eight miles east of Montreal that was served by the Canadian Pacific, Canadian National and the Quebec Central. The crew of Canadian National 4-6-2 5293 has Train 23 ready to roll at 6:20p.m. on February 23, 1957.
Jim Shaughnessy

RIGHT
The engineer oils around his G3-class 4-6-2 at Brownville Junction, Maine, while waiting for the eastbound Atlantic Limited on September 6, 1955. This was CPR's International of Maine division that connected Montreal with the port of St. John by running directly across Maine.
Jim Shaughnessy

BELOW

Another Saturday night, and the Canadian National Railway crew of 4-8-4 6258 leans against the depot at Brockville, Ontario, on August 23, 1958. Brockville is located on the Montreal-Kingston-Toronto main line, and the Union Station here is served by both CNR and Canadian Pacific. Steam-era railroading takes on an entirely different look at night, and we are fortunate that the photographers of that era were so diligent in recording the nocturnal ramblings of the railroads and railroaders.
Jim Shaughnessy

RIGHT

Crews had to inspect and maintain their locomotive on the road. Here, the engineer is checking the temperature of the No.1 axle on Canadian Pacific 4-6-4 2850, the Royal Hudson, at Montreal in July 1958. The engineer is dwarfed by the six-foot-three-inch driving wheels. The 2850 earned its title when it hauled the Royal party across Canada in 1939. Note that the rod within the curved combination link near the engineer's head is all the way down, indicating that the locomotive is in full forward gear. Railroaders do take chances.
Jim Shaughnessy

ABOVE
The Canadian was the pride of the Canadian Pacific, linking Montreal and Toronto in the east with Vancouver on the Pacific coast. In the Rocky Mountains it traversed some of the most spectacular scenery in the world available to a railroad car. On July 29, 1972, at Lake Louise, Alberta, Train No.1 had a matched A-B-A consist of F9s pulling an eleven-car consist and a head-end boxcar. Signature of the Canadian was the luxurious "Park" series of cars that punctuated each consist.
Robert R. Bahrs

RIGHT
A quartet of Fairbanks-Morse units rolls an eastbound freight over the trestle crossing the Kettle River near Cascade, British Columbia, on July 27, 1972. The consist is from the previous day's westbound Train 87 that has been turned, and H16-44 8556 has been added. Canadian Pacific's H16-44s were all built to run long hood forward, but in the 1960s the control stands were reversed for short-hood-leading operation for better visibility.
Robert R. Bahrs

ABOVE
On July 29, 1972, the eastbound Canadian, Train No.2, had a more unusual locomotive consist as it skirted along the Bow River between Banff and Calgary, Alberta. Canadian Pacific bought the streamlined stainless steel consist in the 1950s in a vain attempt to lure air passengers to the rails.
Robert R. Bahrs

RIGHT
Four vintage F-units run by the Montreal Urban Community Transportation Commission (MUCTC), pictured in October 1985. Always painted in a modern scheme, the Fs were two-tone blue-and-white during the 1980s but are now painted silver with blue stripes and nose heralds.
Doug Koontz

RIGHT

A BC Rail freight train heads south along Howe Sound at Porteau Cove, British Columbia, with an SD40-2 and an M420 for motive power; just under twenty-six miles remains of the journey to North Vancouver. The Howe Sound coast is quite rugged; the road and the railway share the same rocky shelf for most of the thirty miles between Horseshoe Bay and Squamish. At North Vancouver, BC Rail interchanges cars with both Canadian National and Canadian Pacific railroads, as well as the British Columbia Electric Railway.

Doug Koontz

ABOVE

Modern railroading in Canada is typified by this scene of a Canadian National grain train winding its way west along the Thompson River at Spences Bridge, British Columbia. Trailing the SD60 in the lead is a string of cylindrical covered hoppers that are uniquely Canadian. During 1995 Canadian National was privatized in the largest public stock offering in history.
Doug Koontz

LEFT

BC Rail was a favorite of train watchers because of its rugged scenery, and because it operated a fleet of Montreal Locomotive Works M630s in a colorful red-white-and-blue livery. The leading two locomotives on this southbound string of boxcars are M630s 718 and 705, shown on August 23, 1989, rounding the curve at Glen Fraser, British Columbia, fifteen miles north of Lillooet.
Doug Koontz

THE PRESENT & THE FUTURE

The future for railroading promises to be bright—and lucrative, as mega-mergers bring down costs and keep profits strong. Technology is available or in the pipeline which is improving everything from rail steels to signaling to air brakes. Even the very look of railroading is changing: satellite positioning and communications-based train control may eliminate line-side signals in future.

During the 1990s, locomotives hit their practical limit of 6000hp. riding on six powered axles. But microprocessors will help to improve fuel efficiency and adhesion between the wheel and rail. The two big locomotive builders are both taking orders for modern machines capable of 170,000 pounds of drawbar pull.

High speed rail is often talked about. Amtrak has ordered equipment and is upgrading its Northeast Corridor line for 150mph operations. Commuter and light rail is gaining in popularity, and most cities already have or are building systems. Modern trolley-like people movers are picking up where those of the 1890s left off. The history of public transit is coming full circle.

Meanwhile, branch lines cast off from the big roads mean many regional and short line railroads will keep the independent spirit of railroading alive.

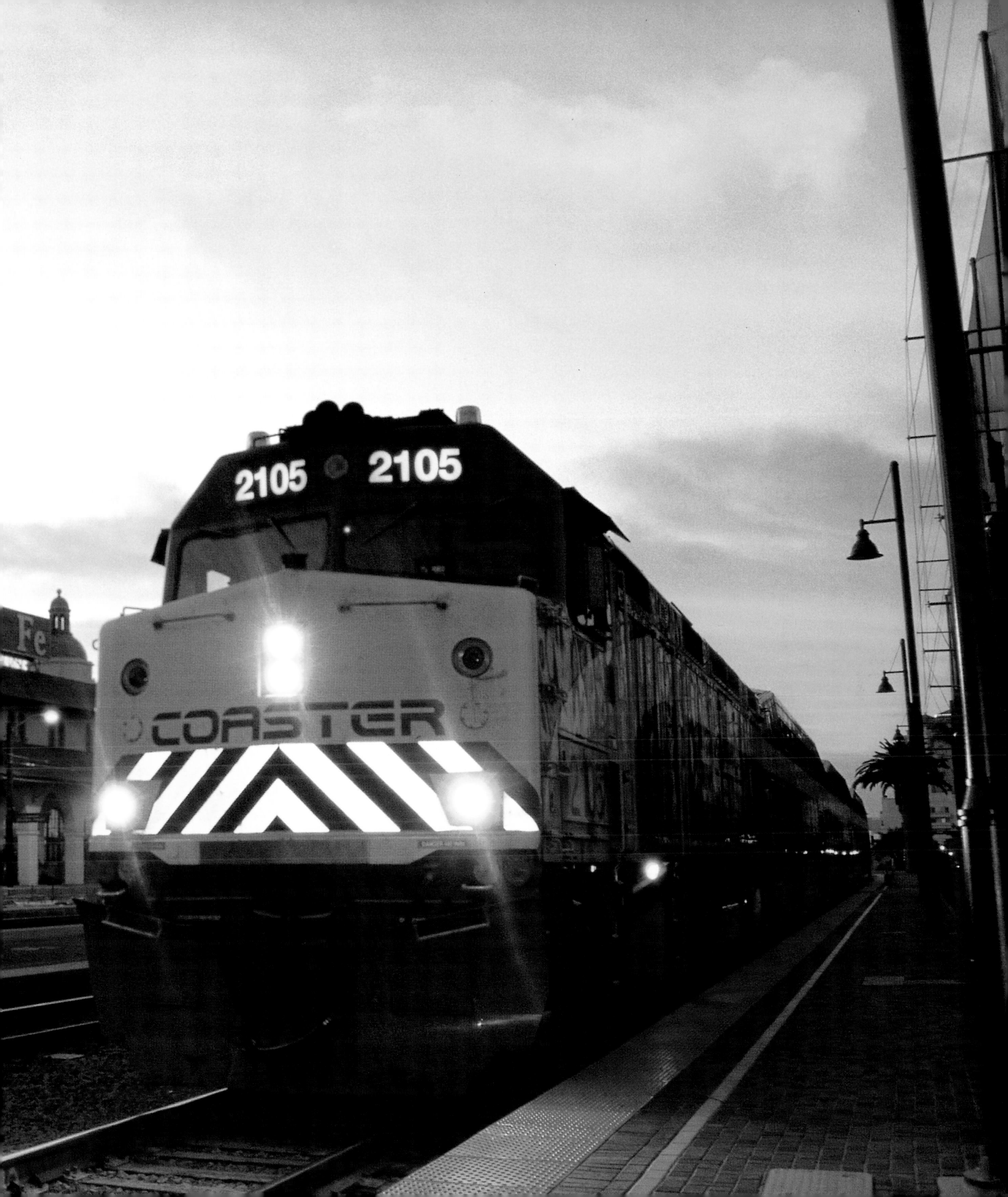
2105
2105
COASTER
Fe

TODAY & TOMORROW

As the twentieth century draws to a close, railroading is entering yet another era. Computer technology is increasing horsepower and tractive effort on locomotives and reducing maintenance. Satellites are improving dispatching efficiency. New materials are improving track structure, and advances in asset management are helping that track last longer. Rail car designs are improving flexibility and permitting better utilization and fewer miles of "empty" running.

In the days of steam and streamliners, railroading was a much more visible part of everyday lives than it is today. It provided the fastest and safest transportation available, and it was the largest employer in the nation. Today's railroads are hauling more tonnage more miles with fewer locomotives than ever before. The fact that they are doing it with fewer people and on fewer main lines has led to a perception that railroading is no longer as important as it used to be. In fact, today, nearly every major city, if it hasn't built a system already, is exploring commuter rail or the installation of light rail people movers. While railroading now doesn't have the variety of equipment, its improvements are exciting.

LEFT
During the late-1980s and early 1990s, Amtrak was testing several equipment designs to gather data to incorporate into its own high-speed trainset designs. Among the borrowed equipment that actually ran in America were the German Intercity Express (ICE) equipment, the Swedish X2000, and the Spanish Talgo trainsets. This artist's rendition shows Amtrak's new design, which will be capable of 150mph running. The futuristic styling is similar to the GE/Alsthom equipment operating through the Channel Tunnel between England and France.
Amtrak photo

TODAY & TOMORROW

Récent developments in alternating current (AC) traction are revolutionizing the locomotive as we know it. While AC current is easy to generate, it's difficult to control precisely. During the 1990s both big builders, EMD and General Electric, had perfected AC traction systems for heavy-haul applications. AC traction had been in use since the early 1900s on trolley lines but it was EMD's F69 and SD60MACs of the late 1980s that taught the builders how to apply the higher torque to the rails. Sophisticated wheel-slip systems compare ground speed to that of the wheels to prevent reckless slippage.

Computers control many aspects of operation, and as a result some locomotives can run for 120 days without a major shopping. The railroads want this kind of performance. In the late 1990s, 6000hp was the maximum available from both builders, but with advances in metallurgy, fuel injection, turbo charging and computer control, the potential is there for a 10,000hp locomotive with a single prime mover.

Locomotive power trucks underwent a revolution in the 1990s with the release of EMD's HTCR "RadialAC" design. Through a simple network of structural "arms," this truck steers its wheels into curves, thus keeping the flange

ABOVE
A westbound Union Pacific train rounds the curve at Clay, Colorado, as it climbs the Front Range of the Rocky Mountains on its way from Denver to Salt Lake City on February 7, 1997.
Joe McMillan

BELOW
This EMD SD90MAC is the current state-of-the-art, with 6000hp for traction. In this scene, EMD 8504 is pushing on a 10,000-ton coal train with two SD90MACs in the lead near Plain, Colorado.
Joe McMillan

parallel to the rail. This drastically reduces wear on the wheel and rail and track structure.

Electric locomotives will play an important role in the future because of the environmental need to reduce exhaust emissions. California is leading the fight against diesel and is already considering legislation requiring alternatives on a few mountain passes.

By the 1990s, Burlington Northern and other roads had already been experimenting with satellite tracking of trains. In just a few years, after its merger with the Santa Fe, the BNSF was experimenting with Positive Train Separation (PTS) equipment that uses satellites to monitor the locations of trains to prevent collisions. This and cellular phone technology will revolutionize railroading. Through uplinks using digital technology, railroads will dispatch locomotives on secure channels rather than public-accessible radio waves; diagnostic information will be sent between trains and the shops. Perhaps the biggest visible change will be the elimination of wayside signaling. The signal indications can be transmitted directly to the locomotive display and printer within the operating cab. MTA Metro-North Railroad has already eliminated wayside signaling on its line along the Hudson river.

ABOVE
Conrail ordered a small
fleet of SD80MACs from
EMD. This pair on a
lengthy merchandise train
are passing eastbound
through the blazing fall
colors near Chester,
Massachusetts. These
locomotives introduced
the isolated cab to reduce
crew fatigue.
Robert R. Bahrs

RIGHT
This Burlington Northern
Santa Fe manifest train is
barreling eastbound
through Guam, New
Mexico, on July 6, 1996.
In just a few miles, this
train will be crossing the
Continental Divide. The
SD75 in the lead is just
out of the EMD factory at
LaGrange, Illinois, and
the trailing General

Electric Dash 9-series
diesels don't have more
than a few trips on them,
either. This red-and-silver
warbonnet paint scheme,
first designed by Leland
Knickerbocker in 1936, is
constantly regarded as
the most attractive in
railroad history.
Dave Cohen

Advance communications and high-speed computers are already making an impact on train handling and safety. After a pair of serious wrecks by runaway trains due to vandals who closed valves in the pipes that blocked the application of brakes, a two-way, end-of-train device was developed that would permit the engineer to make a brake application from the rear of a train.

Later in the 1990s the airbrake underwent a revolution, the first significant widespread change since Westinghouse equipped the industry at the end of the previous century. The railroad industry is in the process of standardizing on an Electro-Pneumatic (EP) brake system. While the air portion of the brake system on each car will remain essentially the same, the command to apply the brakes will be sent electrically by the engineer. This will apply the brakes on the entire train in unison with more precise control than is possible by simply releasing the air from one place in the train. Crews on the EP-equipped test trains are reporting much more control and greatly reduced stopping distances. (Electrically applied air bakes were used very successfully as early as the 1920s but in captive operations with generally fixed train lengths.)

Passenger railroading was growing in the 1990s, and in the twenty-first century the experts are claiming that ridership will continue to be at record levels. Local and state governments are seeing the wisdom of commuter agencies. On some of the newest systems, in Dallas and Miami for example, extra trains and routes are being added ahead of schedule and even established systems like New Jersey Transit and the New York City subway system, are running at full capacity.

High-speed rail in America is a concept that sounds good, but unless Americans suddenly become willing to commit the land, high-speed rail will not have a major presence in North America. The Northeast Corridor between New York City and Washington, D.C. is North America's densest and fastest rail corridor: top speed in 1985 was 125mph in a few stretches and in the 1990s Amtrak finalized plans to upgrade the track to 150mph. Amtrak also announced it would rebuild the railroad between New York and Boston: high-speed, tilting trainsets have been ordered.

It is difficult to imagine where railroading will be in 100 years. Surely, the railroaders of yesteryear would marvel at the locomotives of today being tracked by satellites and pulling trains two miles in length at seventy mph, covering hundreds of miles without having to stop for water or any servicing. But as the millennium changes, railroads are hauling more tons more miles than ever before. The industry has improved its safety record dramatically too. The big systems are getting bigger through mergers and acquisitions and they are spinning off branch lines to smaller companies who can provide more personalized service with less overhead. These small short lines and the slightly bigger regional railroads will ensure that railroading remains colorful and interesting. It is, indeed, a great time to be a railroader, a rail investor, and a train watcher.

Arguably the most significant rail achievement in the world was the 1994 completion of the Channel Tunnel that provides a land connection between England and France for the first time in history. For centuries ferries dominated the English Channel. Built by GE Alsthom, this locomotive for the Eurostar passenger trains travels at 100mph within the thirty-one miles of tunnel. Much of the future high-speed rail equipment for the United States will be similar in appearance to Eurostar.
Quadrant Picture Library

The dawn's early light at San Diego in January 1998 finds a Coaster consist waiting to take the first train of the day north to Los Angeles. Coaster came about through the San Diego County Transit Development Board's decision to provide commuter services between San Diego and Oceanside, California. The stylized paint scheme on the F40PH-2C locomotives and bi-level Bombardier-built coaches make the Coaster trains among the more attractive in California.
Bob Gallegos

The interiors of Amtrak's new high-speed equipment will be clean and comfortable, with a resemblance to an airplane cabin. The plan is to have locomotives at each end of the train, with a modest food service car in each consist. Track improvements between New York City and Boston will reduce the overall running time to less than three hours.
Amtrak

Toronto, Ontario, has been a leader in North America in the use of light rail people movers. Currently, about forty-six miles of track hosts light rail vehicles (LRVs), many of which retain the flavor and character of the trolley cars. On May 28, 1998, during a downtown Toronto rush hour, the trolleys along Spadina Avenue, just west of Union Station, are coming and going among the automobile traffic. Built by UTDC/Hawker-Siddley, nearly ninety LRVs are in service. Toronto also operates a fleet of trolley buses.
Author photo

RAILFANS, RAILROADS & PRESERVATION

Every industry has its enthusiasts, but perhaps no industry has a more devoted following than railroading. The modern moniker for such an enthusiast is "Railfan;" there have been railfans since the beginning of railroading. Even George Stephenson was a railfan. Having grown up near Newcastle, England, he liked to watch the horse-drawn wagons roll by on that early coal-hauling railway more than twenty years before his success at Rainhill in 1828.

Railfans in North America numbered in the millions by the end of the twentieth century, and the avocation manifests itself in as many different ways as there are participants. Whether a rider, a watcher, a collector of something, or an employee of a railroad, the railfan comes from every walk of life. Some of the most respected railroad presidents were railfans, men by the names of Harriman and Hill, and today's Goode, Haverty and Lewis. Even Presidents of the United States were railfans, including Lincoln and both Roosevelts.

In addition to the experience of it, the overall aim of any railfan is some form of preservation, even if just in memory. But while many railfans make photographs and videos, others like to ride the rails or collect memorabilia, and a growing number enjoy getting dirty restoring the real thing.

LEFT

A true queen of the rails is Southern Railway 2-8-2 4501. Shown here on February 10, 1996, the Virginia-green Mikado-type is returning to Chattanooga with a freight train. The 4501 was Southern Railway's first 2-8-2; it was later bought by the Kentucky & Tennessee short line who eventually sold it to Paul Merriman. In 1963, the Southern Railway restored the locomotive, and used it to begin a steam program that lasted more than a quarter-century. The 4501 today is a regular runner at the Tennessee Valley Railroad Museum in Chattanooga, Tennessee.

Author photo

RAILFANS, RAILROADS & PRESERVATION

Train-watchers for years enjoyed their craft in obscurity. But it wasn't until after World War I that the rail buffs and historians began to discover each other and organize into groups, although there were industry associations and labor unions dating back to the nineteenth century. Railroading was still an infant in America when a magazine called the *American Rail-Road Journal* started in 1832. Its corporate successor, *Railway Age*, remains the oldest continually published trade magazine in the US.

But as rail enthusiasts met others, organized groups were inevitable. The first of what would become a national organization was the Railway & Locomotive Historical Society, founded in New York in 1921. Later, the National Railway Historical Society (NRHS), founded in 1935, would grow to more than 18,000 active members in 150 chapters all over North America (with even one in the UK).

Organized railfanning has accomplished great things. Most common of these was to host special excursions over favorite or seldom-used sections of track. In the 1930s, the goal was to operate passenger trains over routes and railroads where passenger trains did not normally go. One 1937 trip flyer reads "500 miles for $5.00." In the 1950s, the goal was to run trips behind steam locomotives before the final fires were dropped. In the 1960s and 1970s, the aim was to run over branches before the tracks were torn up, behind a steam locomotive if possible, but often behind diesels. By this time a few main line steam locomotives had been restored for service, thus beginning a new trend of operating non-railroad-owned equipment. But by the late-1980s, since railroads were no longer in the passenger business, liability insurance had became a serious and expensive issue, and by the 1990s main line excursions were fewer and expensive–but they were still alive.

By far the most significant contribution of the organized rail groups are the more than 200 rail museums that exist today in all shapes and sizes. Each has its own niche. Some of these groups have grown and prospered to the point of owning and restoring main line locomotives, diesels and passenger car fleets. Indeed, more than 1,800 steam locomotives still exist in 1998, and 150 have boilers certified for operation.

It's safe to say that in the 1990s there was more steam running than there was in 1960, the year regarded by historians as the end of the steam era. Each time one of these thundering behemoths enters a town, the people seem to come from everywhere to see this blast from the past. While the adults wax nostalgic about the days when steam was commonplace, the kids are just as much in awe as the adults were at that age. Not from nostalgia—what does a kid know about nostalgia, after all?—but from the very same fascination with the machinery and the smoke and fire that impressed the adults back then. Nothing impresses a child more than a set of driving wheels taller than his or her parents.

The most basic form of railroad preservation is to photograph it. Railway photography began

LEFT
The New Hope & Ivyland is a charming Pennsylvania short line. A nineteenth-century descendant of the Reading Company, its quaint settings and Dutch-styled depots are a natural draw for tourists. The line saw steam in the 1960s, but in the 1980s an investor group turned it into a well-run railroad. Its stable includes former Lancaster & Chester 2-8-0 No.40, a classic catalog 1925 Baldwin Consolidation-type, and the recently leased National Railways of Mexico 4-8-4 which was in the shop for an overhaul. Both squeezed into a single photo during Santa Train season in 1996.
Author photo

ABOVE
Maintaining a steam locomotive can be an all-consuming passion. Here, a Nevada Northern volunteer is trying to remove himself from between the boiler and the frame of 1910 Baldwin Ten-Wheeler No.40. It is the volunteers that keep steam running on the museums and scenic railroads.
Joel Jensen

almost as soon as photography had been developed—in the early 1860s. The pioneer rail photographer was Andrew J. Russell, a New York-born western landscape artist who learned photography during the American Civil War while working for Matthew Brady. After the war, Union Pacific hired him to photograph the building of the Transcontinental Railroad. Russell's resultant work is still considered today to be among the most significant bodies of extant photography. (Many American Civil War negatives credited to Brady were recently discovered to have been made by Russell.)

Technology had improved tremendously by the turn of the century, but photographers were still schooled individuals carrying cumbersome equipment. A few men, like Charles B. Chaney and Fred Jukes, were taking railroad photos then, and their collections are now in museums and offer valuable records of that time. During the 1910s and 1920s, Americans were hooked on postcards, and many local portrait photographers photographed railroad scenes for that purpose. The cards often provide the only photographic evidence of that period. By this time the 4x5 view camera had been invented, primarily for press photographers, and the "box and bellows" soon found its way into the hands of many railfans.

The biggest boon to railroad photography was the invention of the 35mm camera in the 1940s. For the first time regular folks could take acceptable photos. The first rail buff magazine, *Railroad Man's*, was established in 1906 and evolved into *Railroad Magazine*; it began running columns dedicated to locomotive photography in 1931. After World War II, color film and drug store processing became widely available, and soon rail photography developed into a discipline all its own. Railfans preferred color slide film, with its vibrant colors and its ability to be projected.

By the 1990s there were more than a dozen magazines dedicated to railfans and railroad photography. The largest of these, *TRAINS* and *Railfan & Railroad* magazines, and even industry magazine *Railway Age*, rely on the railfans for the bulk of their photography, and once a year Winterail in California and EastRAIL in New Jersey showcase the best work in the field.

Railroading as a hobby continues to grow. The nearly 200 tourist railroads and dinner trains in the United States hauled more than a million people in 1995 for the first time in history. Recreational railroading is booming, and for good reason. The scenic lines in America are as spectacular as any in the world, and each has its own story to tell. Ride one and see for yourself.

LEFT
Looking more like a toy than an artifact, this narrow gauge 4-4-0 is a true treasure of national significance. Looking just as she did in Baldwin's 1875 catalog, Eureka & Palisade No.4 got this way through the love and money of Las Vegas attorney Daniel Markoff who rescued her from destruction. One of her many previous owners was Warner Brothers and she appeared in *The Shootist*, John Wayne's last picture.
Joel Jensen

ABOVE
One of the more remarkable restorations of the 1990s was that of a genuine Electroliner by the Illinois Railway Museum (IRM) in Union, Illinois. Two of these streamliners entered service on the Chicago North Shore & Milwaukee interurban on February 9, 1941, and exactly fifty years later the IRM debuted its restored Electroliner. IRM is arguably the most successful privately run railroad museum in North America.
Author photo

RIGHT
The restoration of railway equipment really came of age during the 1980s. Museums coast to coast began restoring and repainting magnificent pieces at an incredible rate. On May 6, 1984 at the California State Railroad Museum, Sacramento, Southern Pacific 0-6-0 1269 and E9 6051 posed together on the day that restored Daylight 4-8-4 4449 returned from the 1984 World's Fair in New Orleans.
Jim Boyd

ABOVE

Chesapeake & Ohio class J3a 4-8-4 614 is the most modern steam locomotive still operating in the late 1990s. Built by Lima in June 1948, it features the latest in boiler design and roller bearings on all of its axles and side rods. Here, in fall 1996, it was pulling a series of excursions between Hoboken, New Jersey, and Port Jervis, New York, over NJ Transit trackage. The entire twenty-six-car train is stretched out on the Moodna Viaduct, New York State.
Author photo

LEFT

Morris County Central 4039 performs like a locomotive twice its size after an Easter snowstorm in 1979 across northern New Jersey. Cold air brings out the best in a steam engine, as the quickly condensing steam forms volcanic plumes. The 4039 is an 0-6-0 built for the US Army during World War II. Earle Gil bought it from the Virginia Blue Ridge for his Morris County Central (MCC) tourist railroad at Whippany, New Jersey.
Robert R. Bahrs

BELOW

A timeless scene is created each day in Ely, Nevada, when the Nevada Northern fires its mechanical treasures. Ten-Wheeler No.40 was built for the Nevada Northern by Baldwin in 1910, while 2-8-0 No.93 was built by American Locomotive Company (Alco) in 1909. Both are steamed at least annually for special freight and passenger charters. The No.93 is assembling a train of coal hoppers as the 4-6-0 No.40 is assembling the passenger consist for the day. In nearly ninety years of golden sunrises, this scene remains the same.

Joel Jensen

RIGHT

Southern Pacific 4-8-4 4449 was chosen by President Ford's committee to pull the American Freedom Train in 1976 and 1977 to celebrate America's bicentennial. After that it was painted into the authentic red-orange-and-silver livery of the famous Daylight passenger trains. It is pictured on May 3, 1987, rolling through garlic country near Gilroy, California, on the route of the original Daylight between San Francisco and Los Angeles, during the fiftieth anniversary of Los Angeles Union Passenger Terminal.

Author photo

RIGHT

Arguably the biggest prize of preservation occurred in the mid-1980s when Norfolk Southern Corporation restored Norfolk & Western Class J 4-8-4 No.611. The Js were the pinnacle of steam locomotive design, and their distinctive streamlining made them an icon of train travel in the South. In this August 1, 1987, scene, the 611 is barreling at the camera having just exited Montgomery Tunnel through Christiansburg Mountain, exactly replicating scenes from thirty years ago.

Author photo

RIGHT

Perhaps the most overused superlative to describe a steam locomotive in action is "thundering." On June 17, 1990, that was literally the case, even though the two locomotives didn't turn a wheel for hours. In St. Louis, Missouri, for a National Railway Historical Society convention, Union Pacific 4-8-4 844 had dropped a tender wheel onto the crossties while using the nearby turntable. Hometown Frisco 4-8-2 1522 was standing by to lend a hand. The passing tempest didn't help the rerailing process.

Author photo

BELOW
The Valley Railroad in Essex, Connecticut, is another of the handful of short lines that were running steam in the 1960s and 1970s. Its stalwart performer is former-Birmingham & Southeastern 2-8-0 No.97, shown rolling north through Centerbrook during the last sunlit hour of November 7, 1987. In tow are a former-Chicago & North Western combine and several Lackawanna Railroad Boonton Line coaches. The Consolidation-type 97, privately owned by a Manhattan individual, is about to celebrate its thirtieth anniversary on the Valley.
Author photo

BIBLIOGRAPHY

Andrea, Christopher. *Lines of Country: An Atlas of Railway and Waterway History in Canada*, Boston Mills Press, 1997.

Botkin, B.A. and Harlow, Alvin F. *A Treasury of Railroad Folklore*, Crown Publishers, 1953.

Boyd, James A. *Fairbanks-Morse Locomotives in Color*, Morning Sun Books, 1996.

Brown, William H. *First Locomotives in America, From Original Documents, and the Testimony of Living Witnesses*, Appleton & Company, 1871.

Chappell, Gordon. *Steam Over Scranton, the Locomotives of Steamtown*, US Department of the Interior, National Park Service, 1991.

Cunningham, John T. *Railroading in New Jersey*, Associated Railroads of New Jersey, 1951.

Cunningham, John T. *Railroads in New Jersey, The Formative Years*, Afton Publishing Company, Andover, N.J., 1997.

Glischinski, Steve. *Burlington Northern and its Heritage*, Andover Junction Publications, 1992.

Goodrich, Carter. *Government Promotion of American Canals and Railroads 1800-1890*, Columbia University Press, 1960.

Hartley, Scott. *New Haven Railroad, the Final Decades*, Railpace Company, Inc., 1982.

Holbrook, Steward H. *The Story of American Railroads*, Crown Publishers' Bonanza Books, 1947.

Lowenthal, Larry. *Iron Mine Railroads of Northern New Jersey*, Tri-State Railway Historical Society, Morristown, N.J., 1981.

McDonnell, Greg. *The History of Canadian Railroads*, New Burlington Books, copyright 1985 by Footnote Productions Ltd.

Morgan, David P. *Steam's Finest Hour*, Kalmbach Publishing Company, 1959

Scull, Theodore W. *Hoboken's Lackawanna Terminal*, Quadrant Press, 1987.

Shaughnessy, Jim. *Delaware & Hudson*, Howell-North Books, 1982

Wilson, Neill C., and Taylor, Frank J. *Southern Pacific, The Roaring Story of a Fighting Railroad*, McGraw-Hill Book Company, Inc., 1952.

Withuhn, William L. *Rails Across America*, Salamander Books, 1993.

White, John H. *American Locomotives, An Engineering History, 1830-1880*, Johns Hopkins University Press, 1968, revised and expanded 1997.

PICTURE CREDITS

All the pictures have been credited with the copyright holder and source, where either or both was known, alongside the pictures at the end of the accompanying captions throughout the book.

Prelim and section opener picture credits

Page 1: Pennsylvania Railroad at Trout Run, Pennsylvania, 1950s. (*Jim Shaughnessy.*)

Pages 2–3: Double-stacked containers—a 1990s railroading scene. (*Author photo.*)

Page 3 (Inset): A Pennsy steamer leaves the shops at Altoona Yard, 1940s. (*Tom Kelcec.*)

Pages 4–5: New York Central 3060. (*Tom Kelcec.*)

Pages 6–7: B&O's famous William Mason, a 4-4-0 built in 1856. (*B&O Railroad, MARS.*)

Page 8 (Inset): Recreation of an early B&O scene. (*AAR photo, MARS.*)

Pages 8–9: A Northern Pacific Railroad crew poses during construction of the Stampede Pass line, Washington State, 1883. (*Burlington Northern Railroad, MARS.*)

Page 26 (Inset): Northern Pacific A-class no.2611 blasts through Montana in November 1939. (*AAR photo, MARS.*)

Pages 26–27: A CPR train crosses Stoney Creek in British Columbia in 1968. (*Canadian Pacific Railway, MARS.*)

Page 204 (Inset): Southern Pacific 0-6-0 1269 and E9 6051 at the California State Railroad Museum, Sacramento, 1984. (*Jim Boyd.*)

Pages 204–205: Amtrak's San Diego Coaster. (*Robert Gallegos.*)

ACKNOWLEDGMENTS

No work of this size and scope is possible without the help of dozens of people, and I wish I could thank each of them properly in print. Especially the photographers and librarians who graciously loaned the work that appears here. Thanks to everyone.

INDEX